SEARCHING FOR JOAQUÍN

SEARCHING FOR JOAQUÍN

Myth, Murieta and History in California

Bruce Thornton

ENCOUNTER BOOKS
SAN FRANCISCO

First edition published in 2003 by Encounter Books, an activity of Encounter for Culture and Education, Inc., a nonprofit tax exempt corporation.

Encounter Books website address: www.encounterbooks.com

Manufactured in the United States and printed on acid-free paper.

The paper used in this publication meets the minimum requirements of ANSI/NISO Z39.48-1992 (R 1997) *(Permanence of Paper)*

FIRST EDITION

Library of Congress Cataloging-in-Publication Data

Thornton, Bruce.
Searching for Joaquín : myth, Murieta and history in California / Bruce Thornton.
p. cm.
Includes bibliographical references and index.
ISBN 1-893554-56-2 (hardcover : alk. paper)
1. Murieta, Joaquin, d. 1853. 2. Murieta, Joaquin, d. 1853—Legends. 3. Outlaws—California—Biography. 4. Mexican—California—Biography. 5. Frontier and pioneer life—California. 6. Folklore—California. 7. California—Gold discoveries. 8. California—History—1846–1850. 9. California—History—1850–1950. I. Title.
F865.M96 T48 2003
979.4'04'092 B 21

2002192718

10 9 8 7 6 5 4 3 2 1

To my father, Glen S. Thornton

"Men like those I have not seen again, nor ever will."

Contents

"This is the west, sir.
When legend becomes fact, print the legend."
—The Man Who Shot Liberty Valance

PREFACE

A good story needs no excuse for its telling, and the tale of Joaquín Murieta and his bottled head is first and foremost a good story, filled with drama, adventure and mystery—as were the times in which Joaquín lived. The years of the California Gold Rush are some of the most fascinating in American history. Perhaps no other society as politically backward and ethnically diverse as was California on the eve of the Gold Rush has ever been so rapidly transformed, by such an influx of adventurers imbued with such ruthless ambition and near-demonic energy. The tale of Joaquín crystallizes that time of intense struggle and lightning change, a time of radical Darwinian individualism when people, untrammeled by social constraints, could create themselves through impassioned action or through the sheerest drudgery. The Gold Rush, and Joaquín himself, epitomize a vital aspect of the American character and identity.

But it is another theme that makes Joaquín's story so interesting for us moderns. Despite our claims to be rational people who can distinguish between myth and reality, we are still quite liable to confuse them. When it comes to past events especially, what gratifies our deep-felt wishes is too often substituted for what we can reasonably determine actually to have happened. In a previous book I discussed how ancient myths such as the Golden Age and the Noble Savage inform many people's understanding of history and its shaping of the present, whereas these very same people may be convinced that their understanding is firmly grounded in reason and evidence.

Just so with the legend of Murieta: powerful urges have quickened the legend to life and sustained it over the years, and often the mythic gloss is presented and believed in as factual. Of course, historical truth may be hard to determine and is often frustratingly neutral with respect to our feelings and wishes; but a truth—partial, incomplete and brutal though it may be—is better than a lie that happens to be coherent and gratifying.

The story of Joaquín is an exceptionally clear illustration of the limits of identity politics, which assigns individuals to stereotypical racial categories usually based on their being victims of historical oppression. Identity politics is simplistic and reductive, ignoring the astounding complexity of people and historical events in order to construct a therapeutic melodrama whose aim is to heighten political consciousness and at the same time provide balm for wounded self-esteem. The use of Joaquín in the histrionics of oppression has obscured the richer, deeper, more human reality of California then and now. People cannot be reduced to superficial categories, passive objects of implacable, abstract forces. We are all much more interesting and spontaneous than that!

●

I have many people to thank for their support. The staff of the Henry Madden Library, particularly the Sanoian Special Collections, once more were gracious with their help and patient with my demands. Peter Collier as usual was unstinting of support and encouragement. Victor Davis Hanson, José Elgorriaga, Luis Costa and Craig Bernthal helped me along in various ways. Sabina Robinson assisted with references. As always, my wife Jacalyn made the whole thing possible. She also read the manuscript and improved it immeasurably. I owe her and my sons, Isaac and Cole, a huge debt.

The Ride

The town of Three Rocks, with its 108 inhabitants, sits on the frayed western edge of the central San Joaquin Valley, hard against the Big Blue Hills of the Coast Range, a couple of hundred miles southeast of San Francisco. Ten miles from Three Rocks, on Joaquín Ridge three thousand feet above the Valley floor, the three sandstone rocks for which the town is named stand stark against the western sky, shaped like porters bent beneath some burden and trudging northwards. Between the ridge and the town runs Interstate 5, the busy north-south artery that links the Hollywood south to the dot.com north, bypassing the great agricultural Valley to the east that feeds both. Three Rocks itself—a store, a bar and a church huddled beneath a grove of trees—sits five miles east of I-5 on Highway 33, a two-lane road lined with cotton and beet fields and barren land typical of the west Valley, stricken home to tumbleweeds, jackrabbits and coyotes.

On the last Saturday of the last July of the millennium, around six in the evening, Three Rocks is bustling. As trucks laden with sugar beets roar north along the highway to the processing plants near Mendota, a steady stream of cars crunches over dusty gravel in front of Our Lady of Lourdes Mission Church. Families of Mexican farm hands, well turned-out in Sunday finery, troop inside to hear Mass. On a nearby concrete stage a crew is setting up the public-address system for this evening's fiesta. A photographer from a local newspaper roams around, on the hunt for good angles, and a documentary filmmaker and his cameraman wait, their camera aimed to the north. Someone says that a reporter from *People* magazine has shown up.

We are all waiting for some fifty riders to arrive; two days ago they set out on horseback from Madera, sixty-three miles to the north, and they should be appearing any minute down the highway. Their ride—the Twenty-First Joaquín Murieta Horseman's Pilgrimage—commemorates the life and death of an extraordinary Mexican *bandido* who allegedly was shot down by California Rangers in 1853, and whose severed head was preserved in a glass jar and displayed around the state until it was presumably destroyed in the San Francisco earthquake of 1906.

The final, merciless gunfight—worthy of Sam Peckinpah at his most sanguinary—took place at Arroyo Cantua about six miles from where we stand, and just down the slope from the Three Rocks in whose caves the bandit and his gang were rumored to have hidden out and stored their loot. The search for Joaquín begins here, with the riders who have followed the bandit's route to his hideout, covering the miles as he would have, on horseback beneath the brutal Valley sun.

As we wait, I wonder what could motivate people to spend twenty sweltering dusty hours on horseback. Pride in achieving something unique in a high-tech world no doubt brings a lot of the riders out. Those who manage to finish receive a certificate dubbing them "leatherbottoms." Many riders belong to Los Charros Unidos de Madera, a group that keeps alive the traditions of the Mexican *vaquero*—the cowboy—and this ride is for them a reenactment that at least for a few days brings to life a lost age more simple and manly than the present. The filmmaker, a self-proclaimed "Chicano" in khaki shorts and Birkenstocks, speaks of the stolen history of the Mexicans in California, a history that Murieta embodies. Another man speaks up about honoring Murieta's "contributions," including, I suppose, slitting the throats of hapless Chinese miners. But I suspect that a good many of the farmworkers gathered inside the church are just happy to be enjoying a party in honor of a long-suffering immigrant like themselves.

As I stand in the dusty slanting light that signals the start of the long Valley evening, nostalgia is sharpened by curiosity. I grew up in the rural Valley, on a cattle ranch thirty-five miles to the northeast. For a while in the late sixties we had another ranch some twenty miles east of Three Rocks, where the land looks more like the west

Valley, patches of cultivation stark against the dry, barren earth poisoned with alkali. Most of the people living around our home place were Mexican hands much like those praying in Spanish inside the church. My days growing up were shaped one way or another by Mexicans, and to hear only Spanish this July evening, with the cotton fields scenting the growing dusk, powerfully recalls that vanished life. Inevitably the search for Murieta, for the truth of his short life and violent deeds, and the various meanings that may be teased out from both, will be shaped by my personal memories—and the interplay of myth and history that defines my life, just as it does his.

I remember that for the Mexicans I knew the dead were not as finally dead as they are for others; revenants haunted their existence. I came to school one spring day to find my classmates buzzing about the apparition some kids had seen near an irrigation canal—a young woman dressed in white, weeping near the water. Only years later did I learn of *la llorona,* "she who weeps," the combination of bad woman, siren and witch who drowned her own children and now forever wails by riverbanks. I recall too a boy from my school who drowned while swimming across the San Joaquín River after he was discovered burglarizing a country club north of Fresno. For months after his funeral, sightings of him were reported from various Valley towns, so persistently that the local paper mentioned them. In these days of mass-market ethnic hype, most people recognize the "Day of the Dead," the Mexican November holiday when candy skulls and bones of bread are consumed. The ride to honor Murieta clearly reflects a traditional unwillingness to believe that death is final. But will he return the next morning, the morning after tonight's fiesta?

Perhaps he will: the riders will go the six miles to Arroyo Cantua where Murieta was slain; and after a ceremony they will release one dove for each bandit who died, their wings sprinkled with transfiguring dust.

But this raises the question: Can I (or anyone, for that matter) generalize in this way about Mexicans and their belief in the persistence of the dead?

My mother and her sister claimed to have seen a ghostly woman in white, when both were children growing up near Lindsay, a small town across the Valley and hard against the Sierra foothills. Perhaps there is an Italian version of *la llorona,* and such visions reflect a common Catholic heritage. My grandmother was an immigrant from Italy who, like many of the people gathering for tonight's fiesta, barely spoke English. She too believed that the dead visited the living; she actually put a broom behind her children's bedroom door so that any ghost would have to count the straws before entering, and so be detained until morning light sent it scurrying back into the shades.

These musings lead to another question: Who were they really, those Mexicans I grew up with? They arise vividly in my memory. There were *vatos* (guys) like Mico, who had homemade tatoos with the words "beer" and "wine" on his chest, one over each breast; I used to write his love notes to his girlfriend Carmen. Redheaded Joe and I fought to a draw near the old incinerator in the corner of the playground. Spanky once helped me trade a bag of indifferent weed for two six-packs of Coors, which we drank in a vineyard. My best friend at the time, Smiley, spent the summer before high school drinking Coors with me by the canal weir and listening to *Sergeant Pepper's Lonely Hearts Club Band* back in my room. And there were girls I slow-danced with, a few I kissed outside the dance near the alfalfa field, and almond-eyed Margaret, luminous in a white party dress, who socked me when I got too forward.

What defined their identity? How similar were they to the people in the church celebrating Mass? And how do both generations relate to the "Hispanic" of popular culture, or the "Latino," or the "Chicano" of academic discourse? And what is their connection to the "Californios," the Hispanic inhabitants of the Mexican province of Alta California? The search for Joaquín will also be a journey into the complexities and contradictions of ethnic identity.

I look down the road and see the first riders approaching, their horses sweaty and panting. The lead rider is dressed in traditional *vaquero* garb, replete with a sombrero and bandoleros crossing his chest. He carries a Mexican flag. Behind him another rider carries the Stars and Stripes, a young child balanced on his lap. As bystanders mingle with the arriving *caballeros,* the lead rider stops before the filmmaker's camera and makes his horse prance and rear. His brown dusty clothes and pistols give him the appearance of a sepia-tinted photograph from the last century as imagined by a Hollywood costume designer—an image that reveals the symbiosis of fact and fiction which will be a constant in the search for Murieta.

Soon, many horses are milling around in front of the church, raising the dust, so I get in the car and drive to the next stop of the unfolding pageant, the site of the gunfight whose victims will be celebrated the next morning. The road I travel, Highway 33, like the bustling Interstate 5 under which I pass as the highway slants east, follows *El Camino Viejo,* "The Old Road" of Alta California, which itself followed Indian trails and the paths of wild game wandering from water hole to water hole. Unlike *El Camino Real,* "The King's Highway," which linked the coastal missions and is now Highway 1, the Old Road allowed travelers to escape more easily the watchful gaze of the authorities. It was a favorite for eloping lovers and for bandits moving between the *pueblo* of Los Angeles and Altamont Pass east of present-day Oakland.

I locate the spot where the bandit was supposed to have been gunned down only because an awning and two PortaPotties have been set up in preparation for the next morning's ceremonies. I pull the car over and inspect the landscape, which is utterly undistinguished, just more west Valley dullness for the interstate travelers to ignore. There is nothing here to commemorate the fallen hero, but he lives on for the Mexicanos gathered down the road and for the local aficionados of Gold Rush history and outlaw romance.

I make a U-turn and head back down Highway 33 toward Fresno, passing once more by Three Rocks and the church and the horsemen. I have found a vibrant variant of the myth, one powerful enough to bring out the riders in the July heat and the people hearing Mass in the tiny church. And elsewhere in California, Murieta lives on: in the more than one hundred place names, in the numerous legends associated with countless Gold Rush tourist stops, and in the family histories of west Valley and gold country residents, many of whom can recount a family tradition of an ancestor who was robbed by Murieta, sold him a saddle or aided his escape.

One hundred and fifty years of myth and history connect the events of this evening to a past that is part real, part gauzy imagination. I realize once again that from the start, California has been shaped by myth. Cortés landed in Baja California in 1535, and chose the name from a sixteenth-century Spanish romance describing a fabulous island filled with gold and ruled by an Amazonian queen named Calafía. Ever since, the state and its history have been filtered through the lens of romance and legend. The decades of the 1840s and '50s—the years of Joaquín Murieta—especially invite such interpretations. In those years, events converged in California that tapped into the great mythic adventures of American history—the westward migrations of mountain men and pioneers, the Gold Rush, the Mexican War, and the endlessly fascinating legends of the West, the tales of bandits and gunslingers, vigilante justice and hanging judges, and of course the outlaws we now openly admire for slashing aside the niceties of civilization and its effete laws.

These American themes all converge in the legend of Joaquín that was first popularized in a dime novel, *The Life and Adventures of Joaquín Murieta,* published less than a year after the shootout by a half-Cherokee journalist named John Rollin Ridge. But the ultimate origins of that legend lie in the chaotic, violent decade of California's American birth, and in the gunfight that took place near here at dawn on Sunday, July 25, 1853.

The Shootout

At daybreak that Sunday, Captain Harry Love and a few of his twenty California Rangers descended from the Big Blue Hills and rode down a canyon into the Tulare Valley, later to be named the San Joaquin after the father of the Virgin Mary. The sunlight just spilling over the Sierra sixty miles to the east illuminated the smoke of a campfire three miles away.

The Rangers advanced to within a few hundred yards of the camp before they were spotted. The encamped men leapt into action, scrambling for their horses and their guns. The Rangers galloped into their midst with their own guns drawn and yelled for the men to stop. Captain Love guessed these Mexicans were not the mustang hunters he had encountered a few days earlier. These were bandits, and their horses showed signs of hard riding.

The captain started questioning the men in Spanish. One, a young man with long hair and fair skin, who had been rubbing down a bay horse, stepped forward and said in Spanish, "Talk to me. I am the leader of this band."

Love answered that he would speak to whom he pleased, and ordered the leader to stop when he moved toward a blanket near the fire.

At that moment the main body of Rangers rode up. Ranger Bill Byrnes, a gunfighter and Indian hunter who claimed to have known and gambled with Murieta back in the old country, shouted out, "This is Joaquín, boys—we've got him at last!"

Instantly the bandits threw off their *serapes* and began shooting as they scattered in different directions. One bandit, a man with a missing finger, fired twice at Love, one ball clipping the captain's hair. Four Rangers returned fire and shot him nine times, Byrnes finishing him off with a round to the head.

As the other bandits ran and fired, Joaquín dashed for his unsaddled horse, looped his lariat around its neck as a makeshift bridle and jumped the animal down a fifteen-foot embankment into the dry creek-bed.

A mounted Ranger named William Henderson fired his shotgun at the fleeing bandit but missed, then pursued him down the bed of the *arroyo.* Murieta bent over to shield himself with the horse's neck, swinging from side to side Indian-style as several other Rangers galloped along the creek-bed to cut him off. Unable to hit the wily horseman, Henderson shot Joaquín's horse in the leg, but the wounded animal kept running. Henderson fired again, and this time the horse collapsed and its rider jumped off and ran down the creek-bed. Ranger John White missed with his first rifle shot, but after he chased Murieta about thirty yards, one of his rounds and two pistol shots from Henderson ripped through Joaquín's back and brought him down.

"No tire más. Yo soy muerto," he said. Don't shoot anymore. I'm dead.

By this time it was full light, and in the clearing gun-smoke four bandits lay dead. The three-fingered man still had his cocked pistol in his hand, only one round unfired. Two other men were captured, and several others had escaped with wounds.

To prove he had the right bandits, Captain Love ordered the head of Murieta and the head and hand of the three-fingered man cut off, and sent two Rangers with the prisoners and the grisly trophies to Fort Miller, about seventy miles to the northeast across the baking San Joaquin Valley. Love and the other Rangers rode back into the Coast Range in pursuit of the escaped bandits, but their tired horses forced them to leave off the chase.

The Feliz-Murieta Spree

These are the bare bones of fact concerning the battle at Cantua Creek, and even they are not beyond doubt and dispute sown by conflicting reports. Equally disputed are the facts about the crimes committed by Murieta, crimes that ultimately led to the creation of the California Rangers months before the shootout, and that put Captain Harry Love and his men on the outlaw's trail that Sunday morning. Since information about them is derived from rumor, hearsay and the florid reporting of contemporary newspapers—often careless with facts, names and spelling—it is impossible to know which crimes Murieta actually participated in. But he is implicated in at least some of them, and in the minds of many of his contemporaries, the Joaquín killed at Cantua Creek was the Joaquín who had led a gang of cutthroats that terrorized the state between 1850 and that July dawn in 1853 in a series of appalling acts perpetrated up and down California, from the camps and settlements of the gold country to the small *pueblo* of Los Angeles.

California during this time was a world in violent transition. The old Spanish system of government and law enforcement, which had divided the province into districts each governed by a judicial official known as an *alcalde,* was kept in place by the United States military occupation following the Mexican War. But it had been overwhelmed by the influx of adventurers and opportunists following upon the discovery of gold in 1848. The gold country of the Sierra slope, in the old days left by the Spaniards to Indians, became a network of mining towns and settlements that arose almost overnight, populated with dozens of races and nationalities, but the majority being Yankees and Mexicans, the latter including both

Californios and newly arrived immigrants. The Sierra rivers from which the gold was harvested were distant from the coastal centers of U.S. military authority, so that any social order that existed resulted from the ad hoc justice of the miners and ranchers in the Valley who formed posses and courts that pursued, apprehended, tried and executed criminals. Along with the miners were phalanxes of merchants who provided everything from food to picks and pans, and the cattle buyers who supplied meat. The gold country was awash in money circulating in a region with few roads, no police authority and vast stretches of forest and wilderness into which bandits could disappear.

The crime spree associated with Murieta represents only a fraction of the criminal activity plaguing the whole state. But it is better documented than most, an important source for the mayhem being the confession of one Teodor Vásquez, a criminal hanged in 1852 who got his information from his onetime cellmate in San Jose, Claudio Feliz. This man, thought to be Murieta's brother-in-law, was small, fair-skinned and, as was Murieta, a Sonoran.

About ten thousand Sonorans had immigrated to California between 1848 and 1850. The northern Mexican state of Sonora was the "Wild West" of Mexico, cut off from the rest of the country by the rugged Sierra Madre Occidental mountain range, a hard land of mining, ranching and farming. Its residents were continually engaged in fighting the Yaqui and Apache Indians who frequently raided their *ranchos* and violently resisted the Mexican government's efforts at pacification. In the early nineteenth century, the political conflict in Mexico City between liberal "federalists" who favored local control, and the "centralists" who wanted a strong central government, worsened the conflict with the Indians, who supported the centralists. The chronic disorder of their homeland made California a tempting destination for Sonorans experienced with mining and horses. At some point Murieta made the trek north from his home town, in some accounts San Rafael de Alamito de Murrieta, where according to local tradition he was born sometime between 1824 and 1830.

If Teodor Vásquez's confession is reliable, and if Feliz was telling him the truth in his jailhouse disclosures, then Feliz, his brother Reyes, and Murieta were part of a gang whose members—Mexicans,

Californios and Americans—came together on an ad hoc basis, robbed, stole and murdered, and then drifted apart after their crimes. Like most criminals of the Gold Rush, the bandits were equal-opportunity thugs, killing and robbing people of all ethnic groups. And their crimes displayed the brutality all too common in this period. These were cruel young men, daring horsemen riding the best mounts and skilled with the *reata,* the lariat, which they used to rope and immobilize their victims. And they were ready and willing, even eager, to kill when lured by plunder or threatened with capture.

The crime spree began in 1850 at the 17,712-acre ranch of Dr. John Marsh near Mt. Diablo, which now looks down on Walnut Creek, Danville and other cities east of San Francisco Bay. Marsh had come to California in 1836 and purchased the land grant of a Spaniard named José Noriéga. He was an important contact for American immigrants coming to Northern California via Oregon and Nevada, a man of substance who would eventually be killed by another bandit in 1857.

After it pulled into Dr. Marsh's property at the beginning of the spree in 1850, the Feliz gang held Marsh hostage and ransacked his ranch house, stealing guns, cash and gold watches. While there, they killed a visiting American, William Harrington, who foolishly ran out the front of his tent rather than the back, as did his two companions, who managed to escape. Upon leaving Marsh, the gang attacked a nearby ranch owned by an American named Digby Smith and killed three men, decapitating one and splitting another's head open with an ax. Then they burned down the house.

In 1851 the robbers, now including seven Americans, attacked the ranch of Anastasio Chabolla, but were driven off by the alert *ranchero* and his cowboys. Next, near the Gold Rush town of Chinese Camp in the southern gold country, they murdered a fellow Sonoran. In June the gang stole a safe from the Wardis, Lippincot & Co. store in Campo Seco near Sonora. With them was a notorious bandit named David Hill, a twenty-three-year-old New Yorker. Three weeks later Hill, already in jail for beating a man in a quarrel over a Mexican prostitute, would be tried for the Campo Seco robbery and eventually lynched despite the valiant efforts of Sheriff George Work, who was famous in Tuolumne County for trying to get fair trials for men accused of crimes.

Late that year the gang, by now probably including Murieta, was back in the northern gold country. There on the Feather River they roped a traveler named Gallagher and his black servant, dragged them off and cut their throats, all for about $34 in gold. Soon after, they murdered a teamster named George Mather and two passersby who had noticed his abandoned wagon and come to help.

In Marysville, Sheriff Robert "Buck" Buchanan along with Constable Ike Bowen pursued a tip that the murderers were in a camp of Sonorans outside Marysville. As they stealthily approached the *fandango* or dancehall, a barking dog gave them away, and the bandits emerged and ordered them to leave. As the two men were crawling through the fence one of the bandits shot the sheriff in the back. Bowen dragged Buchanan to safety and got him to Marysville, where quick medical attention saved his life.

Meanwhile the angry townspeople formed a posse and pursued the gang to the banks of the Yuba River, where they exchanged fire with them. The bandits' superb horsemanship allowed them to escape. Several other murders, real or rumored, of Americans by Mexicans fueled the panic and were attributed to the Feliz gang. The *San Francisco Herald*'s reporting reflects the hysteria raised by the violence: "A band of four men ... have committed nearly 30 murders within the past two weeks, and [their] path from north to south has been marked with blood."

Stealing horses when their own gave out, the gang made it to San Jose, where they killed a Sonoran gang member named Trinidad, who had threatened to turn them in. Subsequently, Claudio Feliz was arrested for the murder of Trinidad and put in a cell with Teodor Vásquez, to whom he related some of these details. But by February of 1852 Claudio had escaped from the adobe jail and joined his brother Reyes and presumably Joaquín Murieta.

In April, Reyes Feliz was confronted near Sonora by Constable John Leary, who recognized two stolen pistols being carried by Feliz. He arrested Reyes, and with an escort of Americans, headed for Columbia, where the bandit would be brought before the judge. Along the way Claudio and his gang ambushed them. A gun-battle broke out; one bandit was killed and Claudio was wounded and captured, but Reyes escaped. The angry constable was about to blow Claudio's brains out when one of the Americans in the posse, a lawyer named Caleb Dorsey, knocked the gun away. Dorsey later represented Claudio at his trial and got him acquitted.

That same month, Reyes, Murieta and one Pedro Gonzales murdered a farmer named Allen B. Ruddle on the road south of Stockton, lassoing him from his horse and then shooting him in the chest and head. Next the gang stole twenty horses from a Mexican *rancho* owned by Sebastian Nuñez and started off for Los Angeles. The *ranchero* pursued the thieves to the Tejon Pass in the Tehachapi Mountains, about twenty miles to the northeast of where Interstate 5 passes today. A group of Tejon Indians captured Reyes and his men, taking some of the horses for themselves and returning the rest to the *ranchero.* The bandits had to walk the hundred miles to Los Angeles.

The Ruddle family had the money to offer a substantial reward for the killers, and one of the searchers was Harry Love, who would be credited later with shooting Murieta at Arroyo Cantua. Love is a somewhat ambiguous figure, a rugged-looking, six-foot-two, long-haired tough who on occasion carried a sword. To some he was a brave champion of law and order, to others a "large-sized ape ... illiterate and a coward." According to his biography, the reliability of which is dubious, he came from Vermont and was a descendant of Ethan Allen. His brother was supposedly one of the defenders of the Alamo. Love himself served in the Mexican War as a scout and express rider. After the war he discovered a route between Rio Grande City and Laredo, and explored the Rio Grande to determine how navigable it was, though his claim to have traveled the river fourteen hundred miles was later found to be exaggerated. Perhaps exposure of his confabulations sent him to California in 1850.

Love and another posseman trailed the killers for two weeks, finally catching up with them in Los Angeles. Hearing that Pedro Gonzales and another bandit were heading for San Buenaventura, present-day Ventura, they captured Gonzales after a gunfight. En route back to Los Angeles, Gonzales was shot in the head while trying to escape. Love claimed that his pistol had gone off accidentally.

While Joaquín Murieta was living in Los Angeles with a New Mexican woman named Ana Benitez (his wife, Rosa Feliz, seems to have disappeared, if she even existed in the first place), his presumed brother-in-law Claudio went on a criminal rampage in the northern mining communities of the state during the summer of 1852. At Chinese Camp in Tuolumne County, Claudio and his gang cleaned out a group of Hispanic miners, shooting one dead. The next day three Americans were murdered and a storeowner killed at Sullivan's Creek. The gang next showed up near Monterey, where they robbed a fellow Sonoran, Agapito, who informed Henry Cocks, a justice of the peace in what is now Salinas.

Cocks was an Englishman who had served on an American warship and settled in Monterey in 1848. He married into a Californio family, and one of his brothers-in-law was Bernardino Garcia, who was famous for murdering two Americans during the Mexican War, allegedly using them for bowie knife target practice before forcing them to eat pieces of their own flesh. Garcia now was associated with the gang led by Californio Salomon Pico, the cousin of a onetime governor of Alta California, Pio Pico, and the most notorious bandit in southern California, alleged killer of thirty-nine Americans. Since Bernardino was missing a finger, he is considered by many to be the Three-Fingered Jack—a common nineteenth-century moniker for anybody missing a finger—who rode with Murieta and was killed at Arroyo Cantua, his severed hand preserved and displayed with Murieta's head.

Cocks's three other brothers-in-law knew Claudio Feliz from the mines at Sonoran Camp, where they had met him in 1849. They joined Cocks's posse, along with the constable, named Anastacio Garcia, and a black man named John Anthony. The posse tracked the gang to an adobe house on the Salinas River. They quickly surrounded the house, but once again barking dogs alerted the bandits, who burst out of the house, guns blazing. Claudio, seized by Cocks, dropped his gun, but then went for a dagger and was instantly killed by the possemen. Another bandit, sneaking back the next day to steal a horse, was stabbed to death by the Californios who were staying in the adobe house.

During this time Joaquín was in Los Angeles, where at some point he was joined again by Reyes Feliz. Both men were perhaps active with the Salomon Pico gang that was stealing horses and robbing travelers between Los Angeles and San Jose. That fall, Joaquín was implicated in the murder of General Joshua Bean, whose younger brother would later become famous in Langtry, Texas, as Judge Roy Bean, the "Law West of the Pecos." General Bean had moved to San Gabriel in 1852, and owned a *rancho* and a saloon in a corner of the abandoned mission. He had been instrumental in squelching the depredations of a band of Paiute Indians that was raiding Los Angeles area *ranchos.*

One night in November, Murieta and his lover Ana Benitez were in San Gabriel, nine miles east of Los Angeles, to watch a performance of Mexican acrobats called *maroma.* That same night Bean was shot at close range while walking home, and died the next day. A week later Ana Benitez was arrested and questioned about her ties to the Pico gang. Benitez admitted that she was Murieta's mistress and that he was a member of Pico's band, but she denied he had killed Bean. Several bandits were arrested. Under further questioning, Benitez fingered Cipriano Sandoval, who allegedly killed Bean because he had been manhandling an Indian woman.

During the dragnet, Reyes Feliz was picked up, along with Sandoval and Benito Lopez. Murieta had escaped, heading for the San Joaquin Valley to sell some stolen horses. Reyes confessed to crimes he and Murieta and Pedro Gonzales had committed, including killing a Mexican at Sonora who had threatened an American friend of Reyes. Reyes also tried to pin Bean's murder on Murieta. After a trial, Reyes was hanged, and a few days later so too were Sandoval and Lopez. Although Murieta did not kill Bean, the reporting of the crimes and the publication of Reyes's confession, printed by newspapers in December of 1852, first established Murieta's public identity.

By January of 1853 Murieta was back in the northern gold country, where he and his gang emerged as the principal suspects in a bloody rampage throughout the mines. Their victims were mainly Chinese immigrants.

Starting in 1852, at least twenty thousand Chinese men had begun their immigration to California, many settling in the southern mines, where they successfully worked diggings other miners had abandoned as played out. Their success, and the marked differences in appearance and dress of the "Celestials," as they were usually called, made them the targets of thieves and robbers, and eventually of another Foreign Miners Tax. The Chinese aversion to confrontation—most were indentured to Chinese merchants and worked under bosses rather than as independent miners—also made them tempting victims for predatory bandits.

Murieta's entrance onto the stage of legend began at Yaqui Camp in Calaveras County. Three men attacked two tents of Chinese miners, killing one named Ah Kop when he resisted. Four more men, Americans and Chinese, were killed a few days later.

A posse headed by Constable Charles H. Ellis caught up with the gang, now numbering ten, on a hill near Yaqui Camp. The posse charged up the hill, shooting as they ran, and the bandits daringly charged down, exchanging gunfire. The gang escaped and rode through Yaqui Camp, firing at Americans and killing one named John Carter; and that same night they attacked the Phoenix Quartz Mill on O'Neil Creek east of Yaqui Camp. Two guards were killed, but one gang member was wounded and abandoned by his comrades.

Over three hundred miners assembled, and a posse followed a trail of blood that led them to the wounded bandit, who before he was lynched named Murieta as the gang's leader. Three other Mexicans, suspects in earlier crimes, were lynched as well.

These murders, and five more blamed on Joaquín's gang, inspired several vigilante groups and mass meetings, resulting in innocent Mexicans and other Hispanic immigrants being driven from the area. One newspaper article, published a few days after the Yaqui Camp lynchings described above, frankly reported that "the entire Mexican population has been driven from San Andreas and the forks of the Calaveras. . . . If an American meets a Mexican he takes his horse, his arms, and bids him to leave."

By February the bandits had crossed the Mokelumne River and raided a Chinese camp on the Consumnes River. With another posse hot on their trail, the gang looted two more Chinese camps. After a few days, the posse followed the trail of some stolen horses to Fiddletown. There they surprised three Mexicans who immediately lit out on a horse, the one afoot holding on to the animal's tail. The possemen fired and perhaps wounded the bandit in the cheek, but all three escaped. The next day near the town of Jackson, two more Chinese were murdered, as was an American butcher named Joseph Lake. The enraged citizens got together and offered a reward of $1,000 for Joaquín dead or alive. Following a tip from a Mexican woman, a posse surrounded the Mexican camp of Ophir and captured a man named Antonio Valencia, who was identified by a Chinese miner as one of the gang. Valencia admitted that he rode with the bandits but denied he had killed anyone. Then he was hanged.

From that point on, every murder and robbery was attributed to the ubiquitous Joaquín, the newspapers whipping up hysteria by presenting unsubstantiated rumors as fact. In late February the bandits committed a daring string of murders and robberies, some while a posse was literally on their heels. This posse was led by Sheriff Charles Clarke of Calaveras County, who had fought with the Texans at the Battle of San Jacinto and had been a prisoner of war in Mexico. Clarke and five men began scouring the Mexican camps in Amador County. A few days into their search they learned that during the course of a robbery two Chinese and an American miner had been murdered near Rich Gulch.

Off in pursuit, the posse came upon another Chinese camp just as it was being assaulted—the possemen were close enough to hear the gunshots. In the camp they found three Chinese dead and five seriously wounded, but the gunmen had fled.

The next morning, the posse continued to follow a trail of plundered Chinese camps. That evening while resting their horses on a hill near the Stanislaus River, the possemen actually witnessed the gang robbing some Chinese three-quarters of a mile away. The robbers—"five well dressed Mexicans, well armed and mounted on beautiful animals," according to Clarke in a newspaper interview—saw the posse, but coolly kept to their business until the pursuers were half a mile away and then escaped, trusting in their superior mounts and horsemanship. The weary posse returned empty-handed. In less than a day and with a posse in hot pursuit, these ruthless men had murdered sixteen people.

This string of atrocities further enflamed the panic already gripping all of northern California. The report by one Calaveras County paper on the first Chinese murders is typical in its heated rhetoric: "Again has the infamous band of robbers that infests this country committed bold and heartless murders and robberies: again have the peaceful and innocent been stricken down by the hands of a ruthless gang, who have so often stained their footsteps with blood." The *San Joaquin Republican* likewise painted the crimes of the outlaws in garish colors: "Neither in the pages of romance nor in the authentic annals of history have we found a robber whose career has been marked with atrocities half so dreadful as that of Joaquin Carrillo." Whether the surname Carrillo belongs to Joaquín Murieta or refers to another bandit active at the time is a matter of continuing dispute.

In any event, every robbery and murder and gun-battle was now laid at the feet of "Joaquín," and the clamor for action was growing. From May to July he was reported busy in several different parts of the state simultaneously. In May he was sighted in San Luis Obispo, "rusticating," as a newspaper reported, "on one of the ranches, surrounded by a party of some fifteen or eighteen of his confederates, armed to the teeth." He was also accused of killing four men in Vallecito near Stockton while at the same time he was supposed to be south of San Diego driving thirty stolen horses to Baja California. As the *Los Angeles Star* sneered, Joaquín "was in four counties and ten townships in the same day." He was supposedly seen in Hornitos, a Mexican community in the Sierra foothills, drinking and betting at monte, and was said to have got so out of hand that three of his band had to drag him away. Another rumor had him in two gunfights at a *fandango* near Quartzburg, and still another credited him with the murder of five French miners at Bear Creek. And yet another tale claimed that he had killed thirteen Americans and twenty-eight Chinese in one night.

Joaquín's ubiquity was explained by the confession of a wounded bandit captured near Angel's Camp, who said before he was hanged that Joaquín commanded an organized, statewide network. This man also said that Claudio and Reyes were Joaquín's lieutenants, both of whom had been dead for months, which raises questions about the informant's reliability. Yet this rumor of a *bandido* syndicate, added to the others then rampant, fueled the demands for state action. Clearly, amateurs and volunteers were no match for such implacable killers, and such daring and skillful riders.

The public demand for action—including two petitions signed by citizens of Mariposa County and delivered to the capital at Benicia by, interestingly enough, Harry Love—finally resulted in a bill signed May 17 that authorized the creation of the California Rangers. They were to pursue the bandits for three months under the leadership of Harry Love, chosen presumably for his bravery, knowledge of the area and experience in border warfare. The Rangers were obviously inspired by the Texas Rangers, who for years had policed the border badlands where Mexican and Yankee often violently clashed.

Much of the subsequent newspaper coverage of the California Rangers and the battle at Cantua Creek, as well as reporting about the identities of the men killed there, must be understood in the context of state politics and political patronage. This was a time when the California government, filled with hard-drinking and hard-gambling opportunists, was notoriously corrupt and nearly three million dollars in debt. The Democratic governor John Bigler and some legislators were accused of appointing cronies to lucrative state sinecures such as flour inspector and census taker; likewise, the San Francisco Waterfront Extension Act was a boondoggle designed to enrich a few speculators. The publisher of the *Stockton Republican,* a staunch supporter of Governor Bigler, later snagged a printing contract that earned him $60,000 in a single year. Since the petitions from Mariposa demanding action against the bandit were filled with the names of Democratic office-holders or office-seekers, many of the governor's critics saw the Joaquín legislation as just another bit of partisan patronage cooked up by the ambitious Harry Love.

Bigler's biggest enemy in the press was the *San Francisco Alta California,* which claimed that the governor and his minions had "fleeced" Californians "to fill the pockets of indolent officials, or to furnish fat jobs for those brawling hangers-on of party." In subsequent months the *Alta* would be a fierce critic of Love and the "Joquín War." Beneficiaries of Bigler's largess, on the other hand, such as the *Stockton Republican* would lavish praise on the Rangers and accept their claim to have killed the notorious badman. The commissioning of the Rangers, who were each granted a monthly salary of $150, and their subsequent activities were thus occasions of praise or blame depending on the party loyalties of the newspaper in question.

The bill named five "Joaquíns" as commanders of the gang: Muriati, Ocomorenia, Valenzuela, Botellier and Carillo. A Californio legislator, Antonio Maria de la Guerra, had insisted on adding the specific names to the bill since its original phrasing—"the robber Joaquín"—was an invitation to suspect any Hispanic named Joaquín, a very common name. His amendment has occasioned no end of confusion and speculation among historians about the identities of all these Joaquíns. Most likely the five names refer to two bandits: Murieta, who probably also carried the name Carrillo; and Valenzuela, a horse thief accused of kidnapping a six-year-old American girl and killing her father. (He was also known as "Nacomoreno," or "Dark Indian.") In 1858 Valenzuela was tried and hanged for various crimes in San Luis Obispo; it is not known for sure whether he rode with Murieta. The last name, "Botellier," was probably an alias for either Murieta or Valenzuela.

Harry Love immediately began putting together his company of Rangers. Most were hard men who had "smelt powder" fighting Indians or serving in the Mexican War. Patrick Edward Conner was a veteran of that war, distinguishing himself for bravery at the battle of Buena Vista, in which he was wounded and nearly died. William W. Byrnes had hunted Apache and Comanche scalps in Mexico, where they fetched $50 apiece, and had fought Indians in northern California. Once he was almost killed by a man who challenged him to a shooting contest and then, after Byrnes's gun was emptied, shot him several times on account of a grudge.

The other Rangers were mostly of similar ilk, Indian fighters and veterans of the Mexican War. The lives of six of them, including Harry Love's, were to end violently. Mexicans would kill three, some said in vengeance for the death of Joaquín; two others died in a gunfight in Salt Lake City, another in Nicaragua. Bill Byrnes, who claimed to have known Murieta and who identified him at Cantua Creek, died in 1874 in an insane asylum: his body had thirty-one wounds acquired in the course of a long career as an Indian fighter and all-around hard case.

Fifteen years after the death of Joaquín, Harry Love died of a wound inflicted in a shootout with a German laborer named Christian Elverson. The German had been hired by Love's six-foot, 350-pound wife, a wealthy widow he had married not long before. According to witnesses, their marriage was nothing but "quarrels, separations, lawsuits, reunions, and a separation again." Love supposedly beat her. Suspicious that she was carrying on with Elverson, Love armed himself with a shotgun and a six-shooter and ambushed his rival from behind a fence near his wife's house. The two men blasted away at each other, and when the smoke cleared, Love was wounded in the arm. He died during the amputation.

As the Rangers began their search, Joaquín was being blamed for the theft of cattle and horses in San Diego County. In June the *Los Angeles Star* was sure that Joaquín was somewhere between San Juan Capistrano and San Diego, heading for Baja California. Murieta's gang was suspected of attacks on several *ranchos* during this period, including one across the border in Mexico. Andres Pico, of the famed Californio Pico family, would later accuse Murieta, or at least the man whose head was in the jar, of stealing fifty horses from Pico's San Fernando *rancho.* From there Murieta made his way back to Santa Barbara, where he allegedly assaulted two men and stole several horses. A posse including some Californios pursued him almost to Los Angeles, and then lost track of him. At some point he headed back north.

Meanwhile, the continuing theft of cattle and horses in Mariposa County to the north was likewise attributed to Joaquín. Love and his Rangers spent some time pursuing horse thieves in Mariposa County and later in the San Joaquin Valley. Perhaps hearing the reports that Murieta was somewhere near the coast, the Rangers rode to Mission San Jose, where the bandit was said to have a hideout in a nearby canyon. While he was there, Love took into custody Murieta's alleged brother-in-law, Jesus Feliz presumably, who offered to show the Rangers Murieta's location in exchange for his freedom. Love kept his word, and Jesus Feliz eventually settled in Bakersfield, where he died in 1910.

With Feliz's information, Love rode to the Panoche Pass in the Coast Range, about forty miles east of Salinas, and from there sent out several groups of men to scour the area. On July 20, Love happened upon a band of seventy *mesteneros* or mustang hunters, who captured, broke and sold the wild horses populating the San Joaquin Valley, and who occasionally stole horses from *ranchos* as well. Love returned with more men and after inspecting several hundred horses, found some with brands. They confiscated these horses and pretended to leave, actually intending to track the mustang hunters.

But when Love and his men returned after three days, the *mesteneros* had broken camp. The Rangers backtracked ten miles, made camp, and then set out at two in the morning. By dawn they reached the spot where the Arroyo Cantua descends from the mountains into the valley. They could see the smoke from the bandits' fire curling in the slanting dawn light.

After the shootout that left Joaquín and Three-Fingered Jack dead, Love inventoried the goods abandoned by the outlaws: seven horses with Spanish brands, five revolvers, two single-shot pistols, but none of the thousands of dollars Murieta was supposed to have stolen. Love then sent two Rangers, Bill Byrnes and John Sylvester, with the heads and the mutilated hand in a flour sack, and with the two prisoners, on the seventy-mile trek through searing 115-degree heat to Fort Miller, the site of which is now under Millerton Lake. Along the way, one prisoner drowned while crossing the San Joaquin slough that connected Tulare Lake and the San Joaquin River at high water.

The bullet-riddled head of Three-Fingered Jack didn't survive the hot journey, and was either buried at the fort or simply tossed to the coyotes. But his mutilated hand and Murieta's head, according to later testimony, were preserved in a keg of whiskey provided by the ferryman on the Kings River. (This testimony is doubtful, since the most direct route to Fort Miller from Cantua Creek lies to the north of the Kings River. Other versions of this report put the ferryman on the San Joaquin River.) It is more likely that later at the fort an Army surgeon provided some brandy (or whiskey) for pickling. Eventually, Patrick Connor obtained a glass jar so that the head could be displayed more conveniently. Because the glass distorted the features, the head was pulled from the jar for viewing by means of a string attached to the skull.

A few days later the Rangers arrived in Stockton with the strange *memento mori.* Harry Love immediately began gathering affidavits from people who claimed to have known Murieta, including a priest and a Sonoran who asserted he had reared Joaquín. The head was now put on display, admission price one dollar. From Stockton the head went to San Francisco where it was featured at John King's Saloon on Sansome Street.

Meanwhile, Love collected the $1,000 reward from the governor, to whom he showed the head. (It is highly unlikely he threw it at the governor's feet, as one Ranger would claim years later.) He divided the reward with the Rangers. He also was granted $1,000 by an association of Chinese merchants. The next year the California Legislature, moved by his constant complaints of how much of his own money he had spent pursuing the criminals, voted Love an additional $5,000, but it appears none of this money made its way to Love's fellow Rangers.

While Joaquín was alive and apparently ravaging the gold country, contemporary hysteria and vague hearsay made it difficult to sort out fact from fiction. His death and the exhibition of his head only intensified the confusion, as self-promotion on the part of some Rangers and the machinery of mythmaking among the Mexican people initiated a process that over ensuing decades would increasingly obscure the truth.

Initial information about the gunfight sowed doubt about the factual details. One of the first reports had Bill Byrnes commanding the Rangers, with Love elsewhere; another story placed the fight one hundred miles south of Cantua Creek, at the Tejon Pass; still another at the Panoche Pass to the north. The number of bandits present or escaped varied, as did the number of Rangers taking part in the fight. Very little evidence supported the claim that the man with the mutilated hand was the notorious Bernardino Garcia, torturer of two Americans during the Mexican War, who was known as "Four-Fingered" Jack, since he was missing a thumb rather than a finger, and Love had described the slain bandit with his *thumb* on the trigger. Energetic debate continued over which Joaquín—Valenzuela, Murieta or Carrillo—had actually been killed. All this confusion stoked criticisms leveled at Governor Bigler by his journalist political enemies, since there was no definitive proof that state moneys spent on the Rangers had brought about the demise of *the* Joaquín rather than some anonymous Mexican.

Once the bandit's head had wound its way to the north, such doubts multiplied. Those newspapers hostile to Governor Bigler immediately questioned whether Joaquín Murieta had really been slain, while papers supporting Bigler, such as the *Stockton Republican,* praised "the gallant fellows, under Capt. Love, who have relieved society of such a pest."

Other newspapers scoffed at Love's claims to have killed the infamous Joaquín. The *San Francisco Alta California* refused even to believe that Murieta had ever existed, calling the "romantic chieftain" a "fabulous character" created by legislators and their flunkeys in the press in order to justify a pork barrel "Joaquin war." A few days later a correspondent from the town of Sonora wrote, "The report of the death of Joaquin is not believed here." The bandit was seen "swimming the Taloumne [Tuolumne] River, carrying his head in his mouth." Love's Rangers, the correspondent solemnly asserted, had actually attacked and slaughtered seven goats. According to the *Stockton Journal*, the "reported capture and decapitation of the bandit Joaquin may be a humbug," perhaps with some innocent Mexican mercilessly shot down and beheaded in his place. The *San Francisco Herald* reasonably concluded that since no one really knew who "Joaquin the Beheaded" was, every Joaquín in California would have to be captured and summarily put to death.

Harry Love, however, held fast to his assertion that "We have got the right Joaquin and no mistake." To further substantiate his claim that the bottled head was Murieta's, he continued to gather affidavits from Mariposa County residents, including those from Murieta's former launderer, a Hispanic man who professed to have known Murieta for eighteen years, and a prostitute appropriately named Salome. In August a certain Ben Bolt claimed, "I was well acquainted with many Mexicans who knew Joaquín well, and they all testified to the identity of the head and agreed that this renowned bandit chief was now muerto [dead]." The surviving prisoner from the fight, Ochoa, signed a statement confessing that he was a member of Joaquín's band and that their leader had been killed. But since all the witnesses to this statement were members of the Democratic Party, and several had also signed the petition asking for Love's Rangers to be financed by the governor, skeptics looked on Ochoa's confession as yet another fabrication intended to ward off criticisms that Love's expedition was a sheer waste of taxpayer's money.

Ochoa's identification of the head was surrounded by suspicious circumstances as well. Years later, Ranger Bill Howard would describe how Ochoa identified the head: "A Ranger stood before one of them [the two prisoners] with Joaquín's head in one hand and a long knife in the other, from which the blood was still dripping." One prisoner, who later drowned in the San Joaquin slough, refused to speak, crying defiantly, "Cutaway! I'll not tell!" But Ochoa apparently was persuaded by the bloody demonstration. Interestingly enough, in September Ochoa would be discovered lynched from a tree next to the jailhouse in the East Bay town of Martinez. Some would blame Mexicans angry about his betrayal.

No amount of affidavits, whether truthful or fraudulent, could silence the doubters in the press. In San Francisco the *Daily Herald* published an alleged letter from Joaquín that read in part: "I will, through your kindness, inform your readers of your valuable paper that I still retain my head." The *Alta* again identified the head that was touring the gold country as that of "some plebeian robber," while the real Joaquín "is quietly enjoying the fruits of his adventures, at his native home in Mexico."

Many people in the south of the state were equally skeptical of Love's boast that he had killed *the* Joaquín. From Los Angeles came the report that seven Californios and Sonorans, *mesteneros,* claimed to have been attacked by a party of Americans while hunting mustangs in the San Joaquin Valley, and that four of them had been killed. The Americans cut off the head of one, Joaquín Valenzuela. As for Joaquín Murieta, the Los Angeles paper reported that he was "positively *known* to be in the south on the *very* night of his alleged death." But yet another correspondent from Los Angeles stated that Zapatero, chief of the Tejon Indians who had captured Murieta and his men the year before, had seen Murieta and six men riding north through Tejon Pass the night before the Cantua Creek gunfight took place a hundred miles to the north.

When the trophy went on a tour of the mining country, starting in Marysville, witnesses in every town stepped forward, including the current sheriff and the ex-sheriff, Buck Buchanan, who had been wounded at the Sonoran camp gunfight a few years earlier. They all claimed to recognize the head as Murieta's, as well as the pistol and cloak displayed with it. A *Marysville Express* reporter wrote that while he was examining the head, a Mexican who claimed to have known Joaquín from boyhood identified it as Murieta's by some marks on the cheek and under the chin. In Marysville, Joaquín's alleged sister would identify the head as her brother's. The *San Francisco Chronicle* was not convinced: the head "could only have been displayed by a couple of unscrupulous tricksters the like of which could only have gotten away with this in California." Murieta was no doubt "enjoying the cool breeze of Sonora, Mexico, without his head, since that is here."

Years later the editor of the *Express* would write that the woman in Marysville claiming to be Murieta's sister denied that the head was Joaquín's, saying it belonged instead to yet another Joaquín, this one surnamed Gonzales. She also said that Murieta had in fact escaped to Mexico. Later, in the mining town of Columbia, many people, including a man who claimed to have known him as a boy in Mexico and some of Murieta's Chinese victims, would say the head was Joaquín's.

But in years to come other witnesses would cast doubt on the head's identity. Mary Ann Strivens, who was at Fort Miller when the two Rangers brought the head there, said she overheard them identifying the head as Three-Fingered Jack's, not Murieta's. Another woman, Theodora Arrendabo, claimed that gang members told her Murieta had escaped the gunfight. Still another witness said the head belonged to an Indian. In Hornitos, one Rosie Martinez, who professed to be another of Murieta's mistresses, denied the head was his. "No one knows Joaquín better than the person who slept in his bed," she said. These oral reports would multiply exponentially in the years to come and feed the Murieta myth, as well as much of what is passed off as history today.

Part of the confusion arose from the conflicting descriptions of the shadowy Joaquín before the shootout, and of the bizarre bottled head later. The first description of the bandit appeared in an unreliable and unsubstantiated biography published in the *San Francisco Whig* and reprinted in the *San Joaquin Republican* on February 16, 1853. There Joaquín is described as "about six feet in height, and of immense muscular strength.... He has a dark, sallow complexion." A few days later, in the proclamation of the thousand-dollar reward offered by Governor Bigler on February 21, Joaquín, now surnamed Carillo, was vaguely described as a Mexican of "good address," 5'10" in height, with black hair and black eyes. An imaginative rendition by Charles Nahl, published in the *Sacramento Union* on 22 April 1853, depicted a swarthy, long-haired Mexican with huge, fierce eyes. A correspondent for the *San Francisco Golden Era,* writing five days before the engraving was published, reported that a friend who knew "the Joaquín" said he was a "very ordinary looking man, about five feet six inches in height, twenty-two years of age, and has a scar on his right cheek." In 1868 Nahl would paint "Joaquín Murieta," which like the earlier engraving portrayed Murieta as large-eyed and swarthy, with long black hair.

But the descriptions of Joaquín and his head a few months after Nahl's engraving indicated a very different man. Two newspaper accounts of the head, one in the *San Joaquin Republican* on August 11, the other in the *San Francisco Daily Herald* on August 15, appear to describe the same man. The account of August 15 seems to be an embellishment of the earlier one, which in turn is likely to have followed a description provided by Harry Love or another Ranger who inspected the corpse after the gunfight, since the report specifically describes various scars on the body as well. That specificity, following moreover a list of eight witnesses who identified the head as Joaquín's, suggests a certain measure of accuracy, since such precise and copious details could easily be disproved if false.

That these descriptions derive from a Ranger's survey of the body rather than the reporters' viewing of the head is further suggested by the necessarily deteriorated condition of the head once it reached the gold country. Recall that the head was transported over seventy miles with temperatures perhaps as high as 120 degrees. The horseback ride from Cantua Creek to Fort Miller could not have lasted less than a day, and probably took longer. In that heat, the head would immediately start decaying, and gases would cause swelling that would distort the features. The skin and eyes would darken, making it difficult to know the color of either. A description of the head when it was on display in Stockton confirms the discoloration: "The head does not appear natural, being discolored by the blood that has settled in the face and about the mouth." Once the head was submerged in preservatives, first whiskey and then alcohol, the color of the hair would be darkened. Those viewing the preserved head, then, could not tell the shade of its complexion or the color of the hair and eyes, and they would have difficulty recognizing the distorted features. The two newspaper accounts thus most likely follow a Ranger's postmortem description of the body.

In these two descriptions, Joaquín looks very different from the generic Mexican of Bigler's proclamation. The first, of August 11, estimates Joaquín's age as between twenty-two and twenty-five years. He has a "light complexion" and is "rather well made, and gentlemanly in his manner." This last detail obviously derives from earlier rumors about Joaquín, perhaps Bigler's "Wanted" poster that mentioned Joaquín was of "good address," and illustrates the carelessness of newspaper reporting at the time. So too with the assertion that Murieta was "sprightly as a cat." The report continues to mix description of the corpse with the fancied attributes of Murieta: "He had a keen penetrating blue eye, very heavy eyebrows, light brown hair which is inclined to be curly." After describing some very specifically located scars, including one on the right cheek, the reporter goes on: "He had a high forehead, prominent cheek bones, and his face tapered off towards the chin. His beard was very light, as if he had never shaved."

The report in the *San Francisco Daily Herald* four days later in the main follows the *Republican* description, adding a few more physical details and much more interpretive embellishment. Thus the mouth is "indicative at once of sensuality, cruelty, and firmness," and the hair is "a beautiful light brown with golden tints"—information that obviously could not be gleaned from the severed head's hair, which was soaking in alcohol and thus darkened. We learn further that the nose is "high and straight." The eyes, "now closed in death, are said to have been dark blue, with a keen restless glance, and when excited a glance of ferocity like that of an infuriated tiger." The scar is still on the right cheek—"the mark, no doubt, of some desperate conflict." This scar, also noted in the letter in the *Golden Era,* is a consistent detail and supports a newspaper report from the previous year that had Joaquín wounded in the cheek at Fiddletown.

A few more eyewitness accounts of the severed head only furthered the confusion. In September the *Sacramento Daily Union* reported: "A profusion of jet black hair falls below its ears, while the sightless orbs indicate them to have been possessed at one time of a flashing lustre, such as is common to a majority of the Spanish race, and eminently so to that portion of it with craft, cunning or superior intellectual attainments." Earlier reports had the eyes closed, so one wonders how the observer determined their "flashing lustre." In 1855 Frank Marryat, after visiting Jordan's museum, wrote, "Fancy one's features distorted by the convulsive throes of a violent death, staring whitened and ghastly from a glass bottle."

Once more the eyes appear to be opened. The last detail, "whitened," is intriguing, suggesting that the head had perhaps been cosmetically touched up because of its discoloration. Makeup might hide the scar on the cheek. Again, though, the nineteenth-century habit of drawing morals from experience casts doubt on the authenticity of the description.

Another description surfaced years later, in 1888. It came from the reminiscences of a ferryman, Samuel Bishop, who was married to an Indian woman and was teaching Indians to farm on an experimental reservation. Bishop claimed that he ferried the two Rangers with the heads, wrapped in cloth and willow boughs, across the Kings River. Bishop's testimony, however, is riddled with mistakes—he dates the gunfight to the spring of 1853—and assertions unlikely to be true. First, it is unlikely the Rangers crossed the Kings River, which was out of the way for anyone traveling to Fort Miller from Cantua Creek. In addition, the Rangers' prisoner drowned in the San Joaquin slough, which connected Tulare Lake to the San Joaquin River. If the Rangers crossed the Kings, there would be no reason to cross the slough, and vice versa.

Other details of Bishop's report are suspicious. He claims that when the Rangers uncovered the heads, he "quickly recognized the repulsive features of three fingered Jack," with no evidence that he either knew Bernardino Garcia by sight or that his features were "repulsive," an editorializing adjective that smacks instead of stories about Garcia's grisly crimes. The description of Murieta is consistent with that of the Rangers, which could mean either that it is accurate or that it was influenced by newspaper accounts of some thirty years earlier: "The features of the other face were very light in complexion for a mexican [*sic*] and I recognized it as the head of a dashing and hansome [*sic*] young man who once I had often seen riding around the vicinity of the reservation." The features were "very regular and somewhat pleasing" with "a very small moustache." Again, it is highly doubtful that Murieta had spent enough time riding around a remote Indian reservation so that Bishop could become familiar with his appearance.

Later descriptions of the bottled head would both confirm and contradict earlier accounts. A sketch published in the *Overland Monthly* in 1895 generally matches the two descriptions published in the *Republican* and the *Herald*. However, the sketch shows the eyes open, and its authenticity is not secure. J. C. Cunningham claimed that he saw the head as a boy and said it was that of a "flat-nosed Mexican with a very large, thick neck." Cunningham also quotes one Edward Copper, who on viewing the head reported, "The Murietta I know no doubt had Spanish blood in him, but he was handsome and quite different. This head looked like that of a buck Indian." Old-time California *vaqueros*, however, claimed that Murieta *was* an Indian, as did some Sonorans.

However, the features Copper inspected could have been distorted by the jar, and the skin and hair would have been discolored. Half a century later George Barron, the curator of the DeYoung Museum in San Francisco, said he spoke with three people who had known Murieta and who claimed the head was that of an Indian. In 1949 a gold country historian reported that superior court judge Charles Gottschalk of Calaveras County had seen the head but rejected it as Murieta's because the hair was too dark. Here again, the same factors would make it nearly impossible to determine its race.

Frank Latta, though he didn't believe the head on display was Murieta's, confirmed that Murieta was indeed, as the Rangers reported, fair-skinned and blue-eyed—what the Mexicans call a *güero* or *huero*, "blond." Latta interviewed and photographed many Murrietas in northern Mexico related to him, many of whom were *güeros*. His doubts about the head on display, however, may once again have arisen from the circumstances we have considered.

All in all, the evidence suggests that Love and the Rangers did kill Murieta at Cantua Creek, and that he was a *güero*, not a *mestizo*. Still, these conflicting reports about Murieta's appearance have bred continuing confusion over his ethnicity. Depending on the source, the bandit was a *güero*, a dark-eyed and dark-skinned *mestizo*, or a Mayo Indian.

All the details of this story, however, from the crimes Murieta presumably committed to the true identity of the head, can be doubted or disbelieved because of conflicting, contradictory, fraudulent or uncertain evidence; as a result, these isolated fragments of fact would be arranged and rearranged in subsequent years into any number of versions of the myth. But the crimes of Murieta and his gangs, and their impact on the imaginations of both their contemporaries and later mythmakers, can be understood only in terms of the historical forces flowing together in the decades before Murieta's brief and bloody career, which reflects and focuses them.

History

The Californios, Englishmen and Yankees who lived in California in the decades before the Mexican War handed California to the Americans in 1848 understandably looked back on California's pre–Gold Rush days with idealizing nostalgia. Thomas Larkin, an early American settler in Alta California (the Spanish and Mexican name for the state), referred to those "halcyon days." The nephew of Mariano Vallejo, an important figure in the politics of the 1840s and 1850s, wrote in his memoirs that one could not find "a more peaceful or happy people on the face of the earth than the Spanish, Mexican, and Indian population" of Alta California, the province of Mexico that stretched from the present-day southern border of California all the way to the forty-second parallel about one hundred miles north of Eureka.

Such nostalgia for a lost world is understandable coming from people who had occupied a nearly empty and fertile land with a balmy climate, a population of Indian serfs to do most of the work and a leisurely, quasi-medieval lifestyle based on raising cattle on huge *ranchos*. Mariano Vallejo's nostalgia for the "days when a few hundred large Spanish ranches and Mission tracts occupied the whole country from the Pacific to the San Joaquin" reflects a "love for the simple, homely, outdoor life of our Spanish ancestors on this coast." Vallejo's further reminiscences sound the classical pastoral notes of salubrious simplicity: he extols the "simple and healthful standards of those days," the abundant yields of orchards and gardens, the simple but comfortable adobe houses with red-tiled roofs. There was "much gaiety and social life," and family life was "an affair of dignity and ceremony, but it did not lack in affection." Vallejo explicitly contrasts those lost simple days with "these days of trade, bustle, and confusion" of the later nineteenth century, compared with which the "quiet and happy domestic life of the past seems like a dream."

Yet American and English visitors in the early years of the century also tended to remember Alta California through a rosy lens. William Heath Davis, a seaman and merchant who became one of Spanish California's leading citizens, wrote in his memoirs that "the native Californians were about the happiest and most contented people I ever saw, as also were the early foreigners who settled among them and intermarried with them, adopted their habits and customs, and became, as it were, a part of themselves." The New Englander Richard Henry Dana, whose classic *Two Years Before the Mast* (1840) helped make California familiar to Americans in the East, was not hornswoggled and was rather hard on the Californios, but his captain indulged the habit of viewing California as an idyllic Eden. Once, after asking Dana how he liked California, the captain went on to quote (in Latin) the first line of Virgil's first *Eclogue,* the one poem that has always in the West embodied the yearning for the simple life of leisure lived close to a nurturing natural world, the life the early Californians believed they had found.

But over the years, presumably more objective historians also gave in to the mythmaking impulse. In the later nineteenth century—the years after statehood and the frenetic chaos of the Gold Rush had enshrined, in California state historian Kevin Starr's terms, "recklessness and swagger and competitive democracy"—historians consistently idealized Spanish California as a lost golden age before the iron age invasion of the Yankee with his ethos of greed and profit and his nativist prejudices. From this vantage point the conquest of Mexican California is seen as a violent prelude to American imperialism abroad, and the later control of the state by the railroads as symbolic of the corruption of American democracy. Since California before the Gold Rush lacked railroads, rapacious capitalists, oppressed proletarians, strikes, speculation, monopolies, big cities and all the other evils of the Gilded Age, it could be dreamt of as a lost possibility, the better road not taken because of the primal sin of greed.

Hubert Howe Bancroft, namesake of the Bancroft Library at the University of California in Berkeley, was the bookstore owner and amateur historian who organized (and took credit for) a massive, best-selling history of the state actually written by committee. His multivolume, meticulously documented work became the standard authority for decades and established the state's dominant historical narrative. Though Bancroft was a firm believer in progress and the march of civilization that transformed California "from a wilderness into a garden of latter-day civilization," and though he seasoned his representation with virulent anti-Catholicism and contempt for the Spanish, the old world that was left behind nonetheless retained for him a nostalgic appeal, as can be seen in a later work entitled *California Pastoral,* where he called Alta California a "lotus-land," the "garden of the world," the "world's divinest poem" and the "Arcadia of reality," superior to the Arcadia of Greek and Roman myth.

In Bancroft's view, the potential of this bountiful world was ruined by the Gold Rush, when the "young and lovely woman" California became drunk on gold and greed. Then in the 1870s was visited upon the land what Bancroft called the "Dark Age of Graft," the "dethronement of American manhood, the debauchery of American morals," the enshrinement of "false-swearing, theft, cheating, and overreaching," and the triumph of "manipulators of mines, railways, or grain." The worst manifestation of this evil was the railroad, the "vampire" subsidized by the taxpayers but enriching a tiny elite of speculators who corrupted business and government alike: "Possession was taken by the railroad men of the courts and of the government; subservient tools were placed in office, the ablest lawyers were employed to demonstrate the lawlessness of law before facile courts of law, and so the railroad soon had the country under its heel."

Bancroft wrote at the end of the nineteenth century, during what he called the "fin de siècle epidemic of high crime," when the railroads and suburban development were still finishing the job begun by the Gold Rush of transforming the glorified Hispanic California into what appeared to later armchair scholars to be a busier and crasser and less gracious place. Yet one hundred years later, modern scholars also cannot resist the mythmaking spin, evidenced by the title of a recent collection of academic essays: *Contested Eden: California Before the Gold Rush.* Here the cliché of multiculturalist paradises inhabited by "people of color" but then wrecked by rapacious Europeans is the updated version of an old obsession.

This turning to the pastoral idyll of a lazy life lived in harmony with a bounteous nature, far from the hectic corruption of urban commerce, is perhaps forgivable when made by those living at the end of the 1800s. By then, the coming of the railroads had indeed brought industrial-scale wheat farming, real estate speculation and plutocratic cities, changing the landscape and the culture of California forever.

By the early twentieth century, the mythic influence on the collective understanding of California's history and identity could everywhere be seen: in heroes like Zorro, in Helen Hunt Jackson's epic Romance, *Ramona,* in the campaign to restore the missions and the popularity of the mission architectural style, and in that pervasive, contrived, old-Spanish atmosphere perhaps best depicted in Hitchcock's *Vertigo.* The legend of Joaquín begins with this same welter of longings for a bygone world.

ONE

From their own perspective, life for the Hispanic inhabitants of Alta California *was* idyllic. The first Spanish explorers had continually marveled at the region's pleasant climate and fertility. A letter published in 1603 by the explorer Sebastián Vizcaíno praised the "great supply of game" and "land of agreeable climate and good water," thus initiating the European fantasy of California as a paradise. But the permanent Spanish presence in California did not begin until 1769, when Gaspar de Portolà i de Rovira led an expedition to fortify the ports of San Diego and Monterey. At the same time Father Junípero Serra, a Franciscan monk, helped to start the first mission in San Diego.

In subsequent decades the joint efforts of soldiers and missionary priests laid the groundwork of the Spanish social structure of mission, presidio and *pueblo.* A chain of twenty-one missions, strung one day's ride apart along El Camino Real, the "King's Highway," stretching from San Diego de Alcalá in the south to Sonoma in the north, dominated the best land of the coast and coastal valleys. The missions served the interests of church, economy and state;

supported by military garrisons or *presidios* and independent towns called *pueblos,* for sixty years they were the backbone of the Spanish colonial presence.

The Franciscan fathers who managed the Indians were supposed to transform the savage Indians—who lived, as Father Jeronimo Boscana wrote, "an idle and lazy life, more like that of brutes than of rational beings"—into "neophytes," a transitional stage to becoming "human beings" who knew both the Mass and useful skills such as agriculture. Thus civilized, they would then enter the ranks of the *gente de razón,* the "people of reason," and inherit the vast lands of the missions, which they would occupy as civilized Christians instead of bestial heathens. In the meantime, the labor of the Indians produced practically everything the Californians ate, wore or used.

Alongside the missions were the *ranchos,* huge estates teeming with cattle and horses, Indian *vaqueros* and extended family. Private ownership of land was restricted by the Spaniards and opposed by the missions that possessed most of the prime coastal land. Thus not more than twenty to thirty private *ranchos* had been established at the time Mexico broke from Spain. The new government in Mexico and the Secularization Act of 1833, which opened up the mission lands to private ownership, started an explosion of land grants and the creation of the *ranchos*—six hundred by 1840. Soon half of the immense mission herds, numbering some 750,000, had been slaughtered for the hide and tallow trade. The land that under the secularization decree and the Manifesto of 1834 was supposed to be returned to the mission Indians, instead went to the cronies of the ruling elite. Over eight hundred new grants were awarded between 1841 and 1846 (with over three hundred going to Americans), totaling eight million acres. By 1846, one quarter of California—twenty-six million acres—had been given away; by 1849, families controlled fourteen million acres, with some families in possession of *ranchos* as large as three-hundred thousand acres. These grants by any definition established what in Latin America are frequently decried as *latifundia,* vast estates worked by the same Indians who should have owned them.

On these estates the *rancheros* and their kin, supported by the labor of Indians, lived like medieval lords. The men, born in the saddle, were expert riders. William Tecumseh Sherman, who came to California as an officer with the military government during the Mexican War, reported that Californio horsemen could "pick up a half-dollar from the ground, stop their horses in full career and turn about on the space of a bullock's hide, and their skill with the lasso was certainly wonderful." In spring their great herds of cattle—Mariano Vallejo owned fifty thousand head—were rounded up at *rodeos* and slaughtered at *matanzas,* the offal consumed by packs of dogs and an occasional grizzly bear. Every so often the heads and horns of the slaughtered animals would be gathered and burned in malodorous bonfires, or fastened along the tops of walls so that the long curved horns would deter thieves. So many cattle wandered the foothills and valleys that beef, butchered weekly, was always available for a feast, and herds of mustangs—escaped horses gone feral—were so numerous and annoying that they had to be slaughtered like pigeons or run off cliffs.

The social life enjoyed by the *rancheros*—one of carefully cultivated style and devotion to the senses—has been grudgingly admired even by their critics. Much attention was given to elegant speech and dress, and to foreign observers they exuded an aristocratic air redolent of earlier times: "The feel of the eighteenth century clung to the Californians' knee breeches, long stockings, buckled shoes, sashes, embroidered vests, and queued hair," Kevin Starr writes. "The Californian seemed dropped out of time, possessed of an assured identity which belonged to an older order of experience."

Weddings, religious holidays and harvests were celebrated with frequent parties, often lasting for days. Most large *ranchos* had their own small orchestras of harp, guitar and violin, and balls took place almost every night. Revelers danced the *contradanza,* the waltz, the fandango and the *jota* to the tune of guitars and castanets, drank brandy and jimsonweed juice and played the *cascarón,* a game in which eggs filled with perfume (and later gold dust) were cracked over unsuspecting heads. Less elegant entertainment was also available. A favorite, and very bloody, pastime was pitting a bull against a grizzly bear trapped, roped and dragged to the ranch for the occasion.

The scale of such celebrations can be seen in William Heath Davis's description of a wedding he attended in 1838: "[The reception] lasted about a week, dancing being kept up all the night with a company of at least one hundred men and women from the adjoining *ranchos,* about three hours after daylight being given to sleep, after which picnics in the woods were held during the forenoon, and the afternoon was devoted to bull fighting." As Heath's description shows, Californio hospitality was Homeric in its lavishness. Mariano Vallejo's son, Doctor Plation Vallejo, recalled, "Hospitality was the freest thing in the old pastoral days. . . . Your guests arrived, and at once your house and its appurtenances became theirs. How long they stayed was purely a matter of their pleasure, not yours." Travelers passing through were sent on their way with full stomachs and with horses they would leave at the next ranch.

Yet like the medieval lords supported by serfs, the *ranchero's* life was subsidized by the labor of Indians, who no doubt would have been flabbergasted by Guadelupe Vallejo's estimation of their idyllic happiness. The misery of the mission Indians was real, notwithstanding the exaggerations of the Black Legend, that Protestant-inspired indictment of Spanish cruelty manifested in the Inquisition and in the treatment of the New World Indians. At first the Indians were no doubt lured into the missions by the Spaniards' promise of Christian salvation and peace delivered by a powerful god, not to mention the newcomers' impressive agricultural and military technology. But the culture shock of being forcibly and sometimes violently constrained by an alien religion and a regime of clothes and segmented time led to depression, disease, torpor and an astronomical mortality rate, perhaps as high as 75 percent during the mission period. Indians sometimes rebelled, such as the Chumash uprising of 1824. More frequently they just ran away, leaving the coast for the Valley to the east, with its vast swamp of *tules* (New World bulrushes) into which they could disappear. They reemerged periodically to steal horses, which some of them ate. John Bidwell, one of the first emigrants to cross the Sierra Nevada from the east in 1841, during his travels through the mountains stumbled upon a great mass of bones he thought at first to be the remnants of some mighty battle; in fact they were left by the so-called Horse-Eating Indians. And Indians frequently, sometimes brutally, attacked *ranchos* and travelers, provoking fierce retaliatory massacres on the part of the Californios.

Even after the secularization of the missions begun by Mexico in 1834 supposedly freed about fifteen thousand Indians, their lot was dismal. Life in the missions had rendered them unfit for both the Indian and the Californio world. Those few who acquired some land eventually lost it to drink or gambling debts. Father Duran of Santa Barbara complained in 1846 of the Indians' "scandalous conduct, which consists of drunkenness and the stealing of women and cattle." Unable to pay fines when jailed, Indians were "sold" by the civil authorities to *rancheros* for a weekly fee, of which the Indians received only a third—in whiskey, guaranteeing they would end up back in jail and be available for more work. Large *ranchos* were served by scores of serf-like Indians. Most of the *vaqueros* were Indian, and the *ranchero's* house was filled with Indian servants. Mariano Vallejo's wife had fifty-six: each of her sixteen children had a servant, she herself had two, four or five were employed just in grinding corn for tortillas, six or seven worked in the kitchen, five or six washed clothes, and twelve sewed and worked at spinning.

So the life of Indians on many *rancheros* was not much of an improvement over life in the missions. George Simpson observed of the Indians working Mariano Vallejo's *rancho* in the early 1840's that they were the "most miserable race that I ever saw ... badly clothed, badly lodged, and badly fed ... in thrall, in all but the name." Foreign landowners were no more humane. The Swiss immigrant John Sutter created his own empire in northern California in 1840 on land granted to him by the Mexican governor. His Indians, according to observer James Clyman in 1846, were "in a complete state of slavery," fed in troughs "like so many pigs." Those who conjure up a preconquest Alta California ruined by grasping Yankees forget that the Arcadia of fandangos and courtly manners, hospitality and horsemanship, weeklong *fiestas* and lazy barbecues was built on the sufferings of countless nameless Indians.

TWO

The exploited Indian was not the only snake in the Californio garden. Alta California had always been the Siberia of New Spain, fit only for discharged soldiers, priests, criminals and foundlings. The architect of the mission system, Father Junípero Serra, in 1773 begged the government in Mexico not to make Alta California the "China of exile," a place "for worthless people who serve no purpose but to commit evil deeds." Despite such complaints, few efforts were made to develop the region, separated from Mexico as it was by vast deserts and predatory Apaches. New Spain began settling California in the 1760s for limited practical objectives: to provide supply depots for Spanish galleons sailing the Japanese current from the Philippines to Mexico; to head off British and Russian expansion from the north; and to protect the northern silver mines from the depredations of Apaches and Comanches .

Hence for the sixty years of Spanish rule the province was chronically starved of resources as well as colonists. Spanish mercantilism hindered the province's development as well—trade with foreign vessels was prohibited, and no attempt was made to develop manufacturing capacity or agricultural diversity, leaving Alta California dependent on the uncertain and infrequent supply ships from Mexico for even the most basic necessities. When a ship was delayed, bears had to be hunted for food, and the mission friars had to subsist on half a pint of corn and twenty ounces of flour a day; one friar, writing in 1772, prayed for "succor for these missions ... [for] otherwise we are lost." Unattractive to colonists from Mexico, Alta California—"a society without schools," Starr writes, "without manufactures, without defenses, administered by a quasi-feudal missions system"—was by 1820 inhabited by fewer than 3,500 Mexicans.

Even after the revolution liberated Mexico and California from Spain in 1821, conditions did not substantially improve, despite the liberal ideals in Mexico City and the loosening of trade restrictions. Mexico was no more ready than Spain had been to encourage skilled settlers and colonists, or to provide the necessary resources for the development of a region that was so rich in potential, but which to many Mexicans seemed like "the end of the world." The settlers they did send often came from the jails of the northern Mexican states of Sonora and Sinaola, and more respectable colonists usually gave up and returned to Mexico, ending what the British businessman Alexander Forbes, speaking in 1839 of one such venture, called a "hopeless crusade."

Governmental authority was slight and sometimes nonexistent. The U.S. Navy commander Charles Wilkes, sent to survey San

Francisco Bay and the San Joaquin Valley in 1841, found in San Francisco "a total absence of all government," the garrison "deserted, the walls ... fallen to decay, the guns ... dismounted." Californios were continually begging for decent soldiers and the necessary supplies for the pitiful few who manned the presidios. Resources were so scanty that the commander of the San Francisco presidio had to beg his family's clothes from the governor, and common soldiers had to make trousers from blankets. The soldiers that were sent frequently consisted of ex-convicts and lower-class thugs *(cholos)* who robbed the very people they were sent to protect. When General Manuel Micheltorena became governor in 1842, the soldiers he brought with him—mostly convicts—started plundering San Diego as soon as they left the ship. At Monterey their depredations became legendary; they stole anything and everything from jewelry to chickens, and even robbed pedestrians in broad daylight.

Mexican political rule in California, divided between an autocratic governor and the military commander, with both offices frequently held by the same man, was a twenty-year story of corruption, mismanagement and incompetence that incited numerous conspiracies and revolts. Californios were particularly incensed at Mexico's habit of treating the province as a penal colony. Mexico became the wicked stepmother scornful of her neglected child, and the people of California began to see themselves not so much Mexicans as Californios, and even to view Mexicans as foreigners. In 1834 one group of colonists sent from Mexico, suspected of being the instruments of Mexican opportunists out to plunder the mission lands, was hounded out of northern California with cries of "Death to Mexico" and "Kill the Mexicans."

Further rancor against Mexico was aroused by the centralist constitution of 1835, which divided the country into departments controlled from the capital and governors appointed by the Mexican president. A year later, the Californio customs auditor Juan Bautista Alvarado—nephew of Mariano Vallejo, a freethinker who admired Rousseau and Voltaire and had been excommunicated for reading Fénelon's *Telemachus*—organized a revolt against the interim governor Nicolás Gutiérrez. This last was a military commander to whom the previous governor, Mariano Chico, whose ardent centralism and flaunting of mistresses had alienated many influential

Californios, bequeathed civil power upon his flight to Mexico. The customs auditor issued the proclamation "Federation or Death!" which stated: "California is free and will end all relations with Mexico until that country ceases to be tyrannized by the present dominant faction." A declaration of independence proclaimed California "The Free and Sovereign State of Alta California." The "republic" lasted only a year, most of which was spent battling a counterrevolution of Los Angeles citizens, who resented the northerners' pretensions. Ominous was the involvement of foreigners such as the American Isaac Graham in the revolt, a harbinger of their role less than a decade later in the annexation of California by the United States.

The neglect of California first by New Spain and then by Mexico had other pernicious consequences. The inhabitants of California became dependent on the foreign traders and smugglers who increasingly implicated themselves in the economic life of the province. The crews of whaling ships that put in for food and water, and Russian, American and British trappers and traders hunting and bartering for otter pelts—worth as much as $300 apiece in China—could supply the Californians with everyday necessities like crockery and blankets as well as luxuries such as Chinese silk and porcelain plates, despite the illegality of the transactions. These foreigners had sharp dealing practices and an aggressive profit-taking mentality alien to the semifeudal Californios. In 1806 Governor Arrillaga complained of the Americans that "they flourish in trade and know its value ... [t]he American States sometimes send out ten or fifteen regular robbers, who ... are able to disturb our peace and corrupt our honesty."

During the Mexican era, after the otters had been hunted nearly to extinction, the major source of goods and money was the hide-and-tallow trade. Byproducts of the missions and the *ranchos* with their vast herds, hides were sold to be turned eventually into shoes and other leather goods, while tallow ended up as soap and candles—and these commodities were frequently sold back to the Californios, so that the merchants profited twice.

The trade mainly financed the *rancheros'* penchant for gambling and their voracious appetite for the luxury goods that confirmed their high status and distinguished them from lower-class *cholos* and the Indians. Silk dresses and shawls, lace, jewelry, muslin, glass, cutlery, furniture, even pianos no one knew how to play: all were obtained through the sale of hides, the "California banknotes" that sold as high as two dollars apiece and subsidized the *rancheros'* conspicuous consumption. Richard Henry Dana, who sailed on a merchant vessel trading for hides, reported that "nothing is more common than to see a woman living in a house of only two rooms, with the ground for a floor, dressed in spangled satin shoes, silk gown, high comb, and gilt, if not gold, ear-rings and necklace."

The hide-and-tallow trade, however, created the conditions for the eventual loss of California. The Yankee traders, merchants and middlemen—so many came from Boston that they were collectively called *bostoños*—who settled in California were unknowingly (and sometimes knowingly) the advance column of an immigrant host that ultimately facilitated the state's absorption into the United States. The *rancheros* soon became economically dependent on these traders, who introduced capitalist ideas such as contracts, bookkeeping, credit and debt, notions foreign to the essentially feudal and paternalistic world-view of the Californios.

Yet the majority of British and Yankee immigrants of the 1820s and '30s, rather than trying to change the culture in which they found themselves, adapted to it. They converted to Catholicism, as required by the Mexican government for those desiring to be citizens, acquired land grants, became fluent in Spanish, married into the powerful and wealthy Californio ruling class of cattle barons and landowners, and raised their families as Californios. They became important actors in the drama that would unfold during and after the Mexican War. Alfred Robinson, the shipping agent for the New England merchants Bryant and Sturgis, married into the de la Guerra family, the most powerful in Santa Barbara. Thomas Larkin, later the United States consul in Monterey, found a Protestant Anglo widow to marry and became California's first millionaire, mainly through acquisition of land. Abel Stearns, whom the Californios nicknamed *Cara de Caballo,* "Horseface" (since his features had been disfigured in a fight), after years in South America and China became a trader in Los Angeles in 1829. He married into the powerful Juan Bandini family and acquired a great estate, *El Palacio,* eventually becoming the richest man in southern California.

Merchants and traders were not the only foreigners who drifted into California. The Russians had established a fort and trading post at Bodega Bay seventy miles north of San Francisco, and they bartered frequently with the locals. Deserting sailors of many nationalities from merchant ships, warships and whalers found refuge in California's balmy climate and vast empty spaces. The Californios welcomed them, for some, like Michael White who jumped ship in 1829 and started the first boatyard in California, possessed important maritime skills.

Starting in the 1820s, as routes were opened up through the Sierra, and the "Old Spanish Trail" from New Mexico along the Gila River to southern California was rediscovered, more people began to arrive. They included explorers like Jedidiah Smith, the first white man to cross the Sierra Nevada and the first to penetrate Oregon from the south, fur trappers, backwoodsmen, horse thieves, highwaymen, refugees, adventurers and mountain men—"men of roistering temper," as the late-Victorian historian Irving Richman described them. The mountain men, with their knee-length beards, sunburned faces and buckskins—nothing delighted them more than to be mistaken for Indians—were expert riflemen who in the following decades would play a role in the political disorders that were to come.

An enormous buckskinned trapper from Kentucky, Isaac Graham, who kept a distillery near Santa Cruz where he and his pals whiled away the time matching skills with horses and long rifles, is perhaps the most famous of the mountain men whom a British officer delicately called "a rough set." In 1836 Graham and his *rifleros americanos* rendered assistance to the aforementioned Juan Bautista Alvarado, who drove out the Mexican governor from the north and proclaimed California's brief yearlong independence from Mexico. The unruly Graham, however, with his "insulting familiarity," as Alvarado put it, quickly became an annoyance to the Californio, who in 1840 had him and other illegal aliens rounded up and shipped to Mexico on the grounds that they were plotting an insurrection of American settlers. The foreigners were eventually released, and by 1844 Graham was back in California, fighting on behalf of Governor Manuel Micheltorena against the same Juan Alvarado whose rebellion Graham had aided in 1836. Graham's arrest and exile became known as the "Graham Affair" and was much publicized in the United States. The seeming abuse of an American citizen by corrupt and ungrateful Mexicans helped prepare American public sentiment for intervention in California.

Most famous of the immigrants was the Swiss John August Sutter, in whose sawmill tailrace gold would be discovered. After arriving in California in 1839, he became a Mexican citizen and a representative of the government in northern California. He received a land grant of nearly fifty thousand acres near the confluence of the Sacramento and American Rivers. There he built a fort and compound called New Helvetia, complete with eighteen-foot walls, muskets allegedly gathered from Napoleon's retreat from Moscow, twelve pieces of artillery, and an army of Indians and Hawaiians drilled by a German.

Sutter later purchased Fort Ross, the Russian colony north of Bodega Bay. Sutter's realm commanded the trails into California from the north and the east, and American immigrants found hospitality, jobs and supplies at Sutter's Fort and in its fields and workshops; so many Yankees settled around Sutter's Fort that the nearby river was called the American. The American annexation and the discovery of gold at his sawmill should have made Sutter's fortune. But bad luck, worse decisions and the long, expensive process of confirming title to his land in the Supreme Court after the Spanish and Mexican grants were reviewed by the United States, left him broke, and he spent the rest of his life trying to regain his kingdom, eventually dying in a Washington, D.C., boarding house.

Especially important to Mexico's eventual loss of California were those immigrants who received land grants and established estates, indicating that they intended to stay. By 1846 there were so many such *ranchos*—particularly in the Central and San Joaquin Valleys, where the Mexican governors thought foreigners made good buffers between the coastal settlements and marauding Indians—that Thomas Larkin claimed "a person traveling from San Diego to San Francisco or Bodega can stop at a foreigner's farm almost every few hours, and travel without any knowledge of Spanish."

Perhaps even more important were the endless stream of letters, pamphlets, reports, rumors, books and guides sent to the East, touting the Edenic fertility and unlimited opportunities of the land.

The immigrant John Bidwell, who was with the first settlers to come overland across the Sierra, in 1890 recalled being lured to California by a Frenchman named Roubideaux, who described the land as "one of perennial spring and boundless fertility.... His description of the country made it seem like a Paradise." In 1841 Bidwell himself published *A Journey to California,* which no doubt beckoned even more immigrants with its descriptions of a fertile land ripe for picking from an incompetent Mexican government. By 1842, the Mexican government's representative in Washington, D.C., estimated that a third of the thousands of westward American emigrants were heading for California.

Another influential book about California, Lanstad W. Hastings's *Emigrants' Guide to Oregon and California* (1845), suggested the shortcut that led the Donner party to its famous disaster. Hastings also enthused about the land and its "climate of such mildness, uniformity and salubrity." U.S. government officials and surveyors like Wilkes and Frémont were sending back similar reports. President Tyler's minister in Mexico, Waddy Thompson, told the president that California was the "richest, most beautiful, and the healthiest country in the world." The stream of favorable and inviting reports pouring east helped to create the sense that California's future lay inevitably with the Yankees, who would be better able to exploit this natural bounty.

THREE

The neglect of California first by the Spanish and then by the Mexicans did not pass unnoticed by foreign visitors. Throughout human history, rich natural resources have never been suffered to languish under the neglect of their possessors. One way or another—usually by force—such resources are taken over by those who believe they can better develop and use them, or who simply lust for them. Alta California's feudalistic society, with its Indian serfs and *rancho* grandees, struck American and British observers as a throwback to a sclerotic medieval world in which elite cavaliers possessed vast lands they never improved, oppressing a class of quasi slaves held in thrall to Catholic superstition.

The criticism of the Californians, however, did not reflect just the clash of world-views between "dour, dull and diligent"

Protestant Northerners and "easygoing and happy" Catholic Southerners "given to leisure rather than labor." As we have seen, Spain and then Mexico made little effort to encourage settlers who would be inclined and able to create a viable civilized order. Retired soldiers more interested in spending their latter days in leisurely comfort, along with orphans and criminals, were hardly likely to build many cities on hills.

Thus criticism of the settlers came from Spanish observers as well. In 1796 Father Isidoro Alonso Salazar, visiting missions in San Jose and Los Angeles, complained, "The people are a set of idlers. For them the Indian is errand-boy, *vaquero,* and digger of ditches.... Confident that the Gentiles [the Indians] are working, the settlers pass the day singing. The young men wander on horseback through the *rancherías* [Indian settlements] soliciting the women to immorality." So too José Señan, who scorned the "scant relish for work on the part of the settlers. One is more likely to find in their hands a deck of cards than the spade or the plow. For them the Gentile sows, ploughs, reaps and gathers the harvest." Both of these Spaniards, like the work-ethic-obsessed Anglos later, tied California's primitive development to the character-corrupting availability of Indian labor. Nor were clerics the only Spaniards to complain. Engineer Miguel Constansó, accompanying an expedition in search of Monterey Bay in 1794, mentioned the "territory's continuing backwardness, want of laborers, shipping, and trade."

Throughout the century, foreign visitors remarked on the contrast between California's natural abundance and its indolent inhabitants, who, supported by the labor of Indians, were letting such valuable resources go to waste. In 1792 the British Captain George Vancouver visited San Francisco and remarked on "the inactive spirit of the people," who lead a "very indolent life." He marveled that the Spanish who began colonizing "such an extent of fertility" were satisfied with an undertaking that they ultimately "turned to no account whatever." So too did William Shaler, a New England trader, find the Californios "indolent" and foresaw the region's eventual conquest, made possible by the neglect of the Spaniards, who "have, at great expense and considerable industry, removed every obstacle out of the way of an invading enemy." This assessment continued to be made throughout the early part of the century: the English captain Frederick William Beechey, on an expedition to the Bering Straits in 1827, and the American Navy skipper Benjamin Morrell Jr. in 1832 both complained of California's "lethargy" and "neglect."

As more and more Yankees encountered California in the Mexican period, the reports back to the States pictured the region as a fruit ripe for the plucking by those who could recognize its true worth. Richard Henry Dana's widely read *Two Years Before the Mast* is hard on the Californios: "The men are thriftless, proud, extravagant, and very much given to gaming." Dana rhapsodizes about the natural fertility of the land and exclaims, "In the hands of an enterprising people, what a country this might be!" So too U.S. Army Lieutenant George M. Colvocoresses, who visited California in 1841 with the United States Exploring Expedition, described its inhabitants as "cowardly, ignorant, lazy, and addicted to gambling and drinking." The vehemence of these criticisms intensified during the period before the Mexican War, and not just on the part of Americans. Sir George Simpson, governor-in-chief of the British Hudson's Bay Territories in North America, in 1841 drew the parallel, by now commonplace, between California's natural abundance, in this case San Francisco Bay, and the character of the people corrupted by "the readiness . . . which idleness can find both subsistence and recreation." The rulers and inhabitants of San Francisco had turned "the very bounty of Providence into a curse."

More important for American sentiment, however, were the harsh judgments appearing in Yankee guidebooks and memoirs. Lanstad Hastings's *Emigrant's Guide to Oregon and California* (1845) sneered at the "semi-barbarians" who inhabited California, men "scarcely a visible grade, in the scale of intelligence, above the barbarous tribes by whom they are surrounded." T. J. Farnham, an adventurer and lawyer who acted as Isaac Graham's counsel and later became a vociferous champion of westward expansion as well as Graham's propagandist, likewise dismissed the Californians as an "imbecile, pusillanimous race of men, and unfit to control the destinies of that beautiful country." Farnham also explicitly linked the Californio character to the labor of the Indian, whom they afforded "a base, savage existence for his toil." Decades of such criticisms begot a commonplace exploited by Karl Marx, when he observed that California was snatched "from the lazy Mexicans, who did not know what to do with it."

Long before the Mexican War, then, several nations were casting covetous eyes on California, whose inhabitants they regarded with contempt. The Russians entertained various schemes for increasing their influence. In 1806 Nikolai Rezanoff, chamberlain to the czar, visited California and noticed the success of the Yankee traders. He advised in his dispatches a scheme "to make use of any favorable turn in European politics to include the coast of California in the Russian possessions," as "the Spaniards are very weak in this country" and "on account of their shiftlessness, make hardly any use of their lands." The result was the founding of Fort Ross north of Bodega Bay. Less than twenty years later, emissary and naval officer Dmitrii Zavalishin visited San Francisco in search of some musicians who had run off from his ship. Zavalishin, thinking that the Californios would welcome the Russians in order to counterbalance the advancing Americans, devised a plan for the annexation of California. Back in St. Petersburg he lobbied even the czar, but the Decembrist Revolt of 1825, in which Zavalishin participated, put an end to these schemes. Zavalishin spent his exile in Siberia bewailing Russia's lost opportunity for expansion.

The French also thought California a prize worth scheming for. Count Eugène Duflot de Mofras was sent by the French Foreign Office in 1839 on a tour of the Pacific Coast; according to historian Kevin Starr, "De Mofras dreamed of establishing in California a revived New France, a promised land to which the scattered French populations of the New World might migrate, renewing the lost glories of Quebec and Louisiana." He fretted over the possibility that the Protestant British or Americans would seize California and deny the Catholic faith a presence in North America. De Mofras wrote out an elaborate scheme for a French takeover involving French Canadians advancing down through the interior and French warships seizing the bays of San Francisco, Monterey and San Diego. He assumed the Californios would endorse this plan, since they "were by religion, manners, language, and origin naturally antipathetic to the English and Americans." Though the plans of de Mofras amounted to nothing, such talk alarmed both Mariano Vallejo, who worried that "France is intriguing to become mistress of California," and Waddy Thompson, the U.S. minister to Mexico, who wrote President Tyler that "France and England both have had their eyes upon" California.

The English worried the Americans the most, for they were already closer than the Russians and the French, and they had the naval power to back up their ambitions. Hudson's Bay Company trappers had been active in California since early in the nineteenth century. Several English immigrants were already prominent in Californio society as merchants, traders and landowners. Back in England, California beckoned as a convenient dumping ground for English and Irish poor, particularly the latter, who presumably would feel at home with fellow Catholics. Giving away some portion of California, as was suggested in 1839 by Alexander Forbes, a merchant living in Mexico, would discharge Mexico's $15-million-pound debt to England.

A few years later, the Hudson's Bay Company's Sir George Simpson wrote that the Californians were "favorable to Great Britain, while they look upon the United States, and her citizens, with much jealousy and alarm.... I have reason to believe they would require very little encouragement to declare their independence of Mexico, and place themselves under the protection of Great Britain." The English, after all, were still nursing resentment over the loss of Oregon, and were not happy about the United States expanding even further in the West.

Given the richness of California's resources, the chronic neglect and mismanagement of the province by Mexico and the rumors of foreign designs, the failure of the United States to seize California one way or another would have been an event remarkable in human history. Americans did not need "Manifest Destiny"—a journalist's phrase that America's enemies at home and abroad have caricatured into a dark engine of racist, imperialist schemes—to make California attractive. Nor was the contempt most Americans held for the Californios merely a racist pretext for conquest. Just about everybody, including Spaniards, remarked on the neglect of rich natural assets on the part of anachronistic mounted grandees.

Manifest Destiny and anti-Hispanic prejudice are only part of the story of the conquest of California. Ideas are important, but practical necessity is even more so. In fact, all human history has been driven by the seizure of resources by those powerful enough to take them from those too weak to defend them—just as the Spaniards took California from the Indians, and then the Mexicans took it from the Spaniards. If not the Americans, then probably the British would have ended up with the territory. The idea popular today—one, as we shall see, that has helped shape the Murieta myth—that a racist, imperialist United States unjustly "stole" California from Mexico is a gross simplification of the historical reality.

FOUR

The United States, then, had long mulled over the acquisition of California in order both to possess its natural riches and to forestall the European powers, particularly the British. President Monroe's agent to Mexico, Joel R. Poinsett (who gave his name to the Christmas flower), in 1822 wanted a new border drawn that would give Texas, New Mexico and California to the United States. Andrew Jackson in 1835 offered Mexico $3.5 million for parts of the same territory, in order to acquire San Francisco Bay. The idea that Mexico could pay off American claims for $2 million of losses (suffered during Mexico's revolutions or as the result of official misdeeds) by selling some of her territory was also entertained by Waddy Thompson in 1842. George Bancroft, secretary of the Navy, recalled later that President Polk had made the acquisition of California one of the goals of his administration. The acquisition could be made either by purchase—his "Envoy Extraordinary" to Mexico City, John Slidell, was authorized to bid as high as $40 million—or by seizure if war broke out over the U.S. annexation of Texas. Thus there is some truth to the British officer Fred Walpole's statement during the Mexican War that "for a long while they [the United States] had been secretly intriguing for California." But then, so had the French, Russians and British.

Resentment over the loss of Texas, however, not U.S. designs on California, was the immediate cause of the Mexican War. Hostilities broke out in May 1846 when Mexican troops crossed the Rio Grande, which the Americans recognized as the border, and attacked American soldiers in an attempt to enforce the Mexican government's claim that the legitimate border was the Nueces River about a hundred miles farther north.

In California, the outbreak of hostilities cooled the developing sympathy on the part of many elite Californios for annexation by the United States. The neglect of Mexico and the failures of its inept governors had alienated many prominent Californios from the mother country. Leading men like José Castro, Juan Bandini and Mariano Vallejo looked favorably on union with the United States, as long as they kept their power and privileges. Soon after the outbreak of the war, Abel Stearns reported of elite Californios that "I often hear them say *ojala que toma esta Los Americanos* [I hope that the Americans take it]—They appear to be inclined to any kind of change that will free them from Mexico." Nor was pro-United States sentiment to be found only in California: some northern Mexican leaders plotted to secede, offering their help in exchange for arms, and after the war, five hundred residents of Baja California left for California with the departing American troops.

Yet the war and the bungling arrogance of American intriguers, opportunists and incompetents compromised the opening for peaceful annexation. On the eve of the Mexican War, John C. Frémont, the ambitious explorer and son-in-law of the powerful Missouri senator Thomas Hart Benton, was ostensibly on a scientific expedition to California in June of 1846. At that time, perhaps encouraged by secret information from his father-in-law, Frémont violated his orders and involved himself in the Bear Flag Revolt, named after the grizzly bear that the men put on their flag (and that still prowls the California state flag today). The so-called Bear Flaggers were American immigrant settlers who were disturbed by unsubstantiated reports that the Mexicans were going to expel foreigners and render any land purchases invalid.

The ragtag band plundered *ranchos,* killed a few innocent people and captured and held prisoner, among others, Mariano Vallejo, thus alienating the very Californios most sympathetic to annexation. Frémont declared California's independence and led his band back to Sutter's Fort. The farce was ended when war broke out and Commodore John Sloat, hearing of Frémont's support of the Bear Flaggers and assuming the explorer was acting on orders from Washington, occupied San Francisco and Monterey in July and declared that California was annexed to the United States. The property and rights of Californios were to be respected.

The diplomatic Sloat, however, was soon replaced by Commodore Robert Stockton, a close friend of President John Tyler's, and in the historian Jack Bauer's words "vain, tactless, zenophobic [*sic*], and glory-thirsty," who designated the Bear Flaggers the "California Battalion," thus conferring semi-official sanction on their illicit actions. In August, Stockton headed south to conquer the rest of the province. At the Americans' approach, the last government of Mexican California dissolved, most of the remaining military forces retiring to the Rancho San Pasqual near modern-day Pasadena. Stockton set about organizing a civilian territorial government.

The commodore left Captain Archibald Gillespie, Frémont's second-in-command, to administer the notoriously unruly southern California, which was under martial law. The tall, red-headed Gillespie was ambitious and prejudiced against Spaniards, and particularly disliked the Californios, who he thought were "cowardly and inert." In Los Angeles he set about issuing oppressive regulations, such as forbidding two people from walking the streets together or the selling of liquor without his permission. According to Thomas Larkin, "It appears even from the Americans that Captain AHG punished fined and imprisoned who and when he pleased without any hearing."

Los Angeles was a rough town filled in any case with turbulent malcontents, and in September rebellion broke out when twenty Californios exchanged gunfire with the forty-eight-man American garrison. After some tense days the Americans retreated to a more defensible position, but one that unfortunately had no water. They surrendered the next day, eventually to board a merchant ship docked in San Pedro, still Los Angeles' port.

The Californios set about routing any remaining Americans in the south; but they were merely delaying the inevitable, given the Americans' superior numbers and matériel. Stockton sent two relief forces, one of which immediately upon landing at San Pedro began marching against Los Angeles. They made little headway, however, against the cavalry and artillery of the Californios. Stockton then shifted his base of operations from San Pedro to San Diego while

Frémont marched south from Monterey. Meanwhile Brigadier General Stephen W. Kearny was approaching southern California from the east after pacifying New Mexico.

In December the American forces linked up and clashed with the Californio army at the village of San Pasqual near San Diego, a battle that turned out to be the last glorious stand of the Californio horsemen. When the tired, ill-mounted Americans attacked, the Californios feigned retreat, then wheeled and with their willow lances routed the pursuing Americans, killing eighteen and wounding the hated Gillespie three times, but not fatally. Both the Californios and the Americans then headed back to Los Angeles. In January, Los Angeles was retaken after the Battle of the San Gabriel at the river of the same name. With Frémont having broken all resistance in the north and moving south to Los Angeles, the war in California was over. The Californios capitulated, and California had become part of the United States.

After the Americans conquered and occupied Mexico City in September 1847, the Mexican War was for all intents and purposes over, though fighting would continue for some months. The formal end of hostilities, the Treaty of Guadalupe Hidalgo of February 1848, paid Mexico $15 million—about $2.3 billion in current value—for her northern provinces. The Californios would later bitterly complain that Mexico had sold them like sheep for the slaughter.

Despite the ill will and resentment caused by the war and the arrogance of men like Commodore Stockton and Archibald Gillespie, there was still a chance that California could in time be peacefully integrated into the Union. The prospect of political and economic order after two decades of Mexican neglect and chaos perhaps salved the wounded pride of the Californio elite. Bayard Taylor, who in 1849 covered the California constitutional convention for the *New York Tribune,* wrote of the Californios that "the intelligent and influential faction which aided us during the war is still faithful and many who were previously discontented are now loudest in their rejoicing." The sensible and fair military administration of General Stephen Kearny—whose battle with Stockton over who was to administer California was settled in Kearny's favor by the arrival from Washington of Colonel Richard B. Mason—was a welcome relief from Stockton's highhanded ways. Kearny ordered the California Battalion to be dissolved, and when Frémont refused sent him packing back to Washington to answer charges of mutiny. Kearny also paid restitution for the depredations of the Bear Flaggers, enforced Mexican laws that did not conflict with the U.S. Constitution, kept active the office of *alcalde* (the most important Mexican governmental official after the governor) and appointed Californios to government office.

Kearny's successor, Richard Mason, was likewise just and conciliatory. The integration of the Californio elite into the nascent ruling class was evident when eight Californios, including Mariano Vallejo, in 1849 were elected representatives to the constitutional convention to determine the issue of statehood. Indeed, of the 157 men who served the provisional government from 1847 to 1849, some 48 were born in California and Mexico. Bayard Taylor's prediction that "the future government of the State will soon obliterate the differences of race and condition, and all will then be equally Californian and American citizens," appeared for a moment feasible. But in January of 1848 an event occurred that would change California, the United States and the world forever—and catapult Joaquín Murieta into legend.

FIVE

When John Marshall, a veteran of the California Battalion hired by John Sutter to build a sawmill on the American River, picked up a few particles of gold from the mill's tailrace, he initiated one of the swiftest and most radical transformations of a society ever recorded. Within the year a hundred thousand "argonauts," named after the mythic seekers of the golden fleece, had poured into northern California, quintupling the number of inhabitants and creating what Thomas Ap C. Jones, commander of the U.S. Navy's Pacific Squadron headquartered in San Francisco, called a "whirlwind of anarchy and confusion."

The tiny village of Yerba Buena, soon to be renamed San Francisco, a place of "fog, fleas, winds, and sterility" (as a French visitor described it) that for years had slumbered among the sand dunes next to the bay, in a matter of months exploded into a muddy, bustling, raucous, chaotic tent city. Its "unreal and fantastic" nighttime glow reminded Bayard Taylor of "the cities of the magic lantern, which the motion of a hand can build or annihilate." The mud was so bad that sometimes when drunks passed out and fell into it, they smothered to death. Cases of goods such as Virginia tobacco, which were too expensive to store because of astronomical rents, were used for sidewalks. In the bay, several hundred abandoned hulks, their sailors having jumped ship for the gold fields, served as floating hotels, jails and brothels, or else provided materials for frenetic construction whose noisy hammering went on night and day.

In the first months of the Gold Rush, anyone with a pan, a shovel and the ability to withstand the ice-cold Sierra rivers could find gold by washing panfuls of gravel with river water to separate out the nuggets, a method known as placer mining. The impact of so much wealth flooding into a society so quickly—$10 million worth the first year—cannot be underestimated. All the expensive vices flourished—prostitution, drinking, gambling. Inflation ran rampant: a doctor charged one ounce of gold (about $16) to take a pulse; a saloonkeeper on the Stanislaus River took in $1,000 per day. Indians with gold were particularly vulnerable to price gouging. Thomas Larkin reported that an Indian typically paid from $8 to $16 for a calico shirt, while a blanket went for $48 to $360. Daily wages that were $1.50 elsewhere in the United States ran from $6 to $12, but a gold-digger earned $100—*two thousand dollars* in today's money. Theft and robbery were not a big problem that first year, probably because there was so much wealth to be had with less risk. But soon the volume of both money and men seeking it would turn California of the 1840s and 1850s into the most violent place in American history.

Equally significant was the astonishing variety of men, both in race and in character, who underwent epic adventures on sea and land to reach the gold fields. Vast numbers of Americans, of course, made their way by wagon and ship to California. There were also Sonorans like Joaquín Murieta, Chileans, Peruvians, Hawaiians, Malaysians, Chinese, Australian convicts, French refugees from the failed revolution of 1848, Irish refugees from famine, Irish-American deserters from the New York Regiment, Scots and Welsh. And there were some "in whose embrowned and bearded visages it was impossible to recognize any especial nationality," according to Bayard Taylor, the reporter sent to California by the *New York Tribune*'s Horace Greeley. All were crammed together cheek by jowl on the banks of icy rivers—the American, the Feather, the Sacramento and the Yuba—that were filled with gold that had washed down from the Sierra for eons.

The Chilean diarist Vicente Perez Rosales wrote about the confusing interactions of so many different peoples: "There is stocky John Bull, a Chinaman, a Hindu, a Russian, and a native Californio, all trying to converse. A Chilean and an Oregonian are watching each other suspiciously. A Frenchman and an Italian are winking at a Hawaiian girl crowned with flowers and clad in a blue dress and red shoes." As one can imagine, other encounters were not so charmingly multicultural and serene.

Nor is this surprising, given that the characters of many of these adventurers were not the most sterling. *The Annals of San Francisco* described them as a "rowdy and knavish class," comprising "sharpers, gamblers, and cheating adventurers in every variety of scheme" who were ready "to prey upon the community at large." Hugo Reid, a Yankee Californio, wrote that this motley collection was composed of "Vagabonds from every quarter of the globe. Scoundrels from nowhere, rascals from Oregon, pickpockets from New York, accomplished gentlemen from Europe, interlopers from Lima and Chile, Mexican thieves, gamblers of no particular spot, and assassins manufactured in Hell for the expressed [*sic*] purpose of converting highways and biways [*sic*] into theatres of blood."

Ex-argonaut Alonzo Delano, who gained some celebrity writing under the pen name "Old Block," snorted that California's touted "greatness" lay in its status as an outlet for "surplus wheat, pork, and clothes, blacklegs [swindlers], prostitutes, and vicious" from the rest of the United States. Ralph Waldo Emerson agreed, calling the Gold Rush a "scramble of needy adventurers ... [and] a general jail delivery of all the rowdies of the rivers." A longtime Yankee resident of Monterey, Walter Colton, noted the contrast between the generous hospitality of the Californios and the crude greed of many miners. He wrote, "If I must be cast in destitution on the care of the stranger, let it be in California; but let it be before the American avarice has hardened the heart and made a god of gold." Whatever its deficiencies, the gracious, leisurely lifestyle of the old Californio *rancheros* with their weeklong *fiestas* and elegant manners became more and more attractive as it was swallowed up by the commercial frenzy of the Gold Rush.

No society, especially one like California's that had recently seen civil strife and conquest and lacked a civil government to impose and maintain order, could survive such an onslaught of avarice and ethnic mixing without conflict and turmoil. This hodgepodge of races, nationalities and classes, which included so many rootless men without women, families or civil society to restrain their impulses, constituted the perfect breeding ground for extreme behaviors. These men were driven by greed for instant wealth and goaded by every vice and appetite, swept along by what Bayard Taylor hauntingly called "the magnetism of bold, spirited, unwearied action." Nor was this force easy to resist: "He who but ventures into the outer circle of the whirlpool," Taylor added, "is spinning, ere he has time for thought, in its dizzy vortex."

In short, California during the Gold Rush was a Darwinian place of "primitive and brutal conditions," which historian Kevin Starr vividly describes as "a Homeric world of journeys, shipwreck, labor, treasure, killing, and chieftainship" where the primal nature of man stands revealed. The old world of the Californios, into which earlier American and British immigrants had assimilated themselves—a world full of promise for a truly multiethnic society and a new hybrid culture—was shattered overnight by the forces now unleashed.

SIX

For the next two decades the region would be plagued by brigandage, robbery, banditry, theft and murder.

Complaints about lawlessness and mayhem dominate accounts from the period. In 1852 the *Los Angeles Star* wrote, "There is no country where human life is of so little account. Men hack one another to pieces with pistols and other cutlery, as if God's image were of no more worth than that of [an] ownerless dog." Enos Christman, writing back home to easterners of an incident in the Gold Rush town of Sonora in 1850, casually remarked, "Yesterday one American shot another in the street, and the occurrence was not noticed as much as a dog fight at home." Young men with weapons; a dearth of women; an abundance of saloons, gambling establishments and *fandangos* (dancehalls); a near-absence of civil and legal authority; huge unpopulated spaces of forest and mountain into which the lawless could disappear—these were some of the conditions that unleashed such phenomenal violence.

The first documented murder of the Gold Rush happened on October 1, 1848, at Sutter's Mill—where of course gold had been discovered some months earlier. The murderer was Peter Raymond, a twenty-year-old Irish sailor and veteran of Frémont's California Battalion, who stabbed to death a miner named John Von Pfister. Raymond escaped custody with the help of a fellow Irishman named Quinn, and the two joined up with another Irishman and a German who had just murdered a couple of miners. Along with an Indian named Juan, in December the group rode to Mission San Miguel, sixty-five miles south of Soledad. After the Mexican government secularized the missions in 1833, they were sold off to private owners, excepting the chapels and priests' quarters. San Miguel was now owned by a retired British seaman named William Reed and his partner, a former artillery officer from the Mexican Army, Petronilo Rios.

With Reed that night was his pregnant Mexican wife and their son, a Mexican midwife and her two children, his wife's brother, an Indian shepherd, the shepherd's grandson and a black cook. Incited by the incautious Reed's bragging about his profits from mining and from selling a flock of sheep, the gang hacked, stabbed and shot to death all ten people. They then piled up the corpses and set them on fire.

Meanwhile the noted trapper and mountain man Jim Beckwourth, the son of a plantation owner and a slave who was now a mail rider for the government, had entered the house while the murderers were still there and discovered two of the victims. Sensing the killers' presence, he bolted and galloped off to alert Reed's partner Rios, and then rode on to Monterey to inform the military authorities. The adjutant to Military Governor Richard Mason, William Tecumseh Sherman, remembered Beckwourth crying, "They killed them all, not even sparing the baby!" California, future home of Charles Manson and Jim Jones, had its first mass murder.

Two posses were formed, one of *vaqueros* and Indians, the other made up of three Yankees and twelve Californios. The gang was tracked to Santa Barbara, where a gun-battle on the beach left one posse member and three of the fugitives dead, one of them shot to pieces as he bobbed in the ocean, attempting to swim away. The other three murderers were tried by a jury of six Anglos and six Californios, found guilty and executed by firing squad in a ravine near town after receiving the last rites from a priest. As Gold Rush historian John Boessenecker writes, "The San Miguel massacre became the pattern for much of the violence and retributive justice that would follow in the Gold Rush. The culprits were all violent, greedy men, banded together out of common and vicious goals." Worthy of notice is the ethnic variety of both the bandits and the posses.

Robbery and murder spread through California. Miners flush with gold were obvious prey. Cattle buyers traveling between the *ranchos* in the central and southern regions and the meat-hungry mines in the north frequently disappeared, their moldering bodies found months later. Californian Walter Murray, an attorney in San Luis Obispo, wrote that by 1853 "scarcely a month has passed without the disappearance of some traveler, or the finding of dead bodies or skeletons on the roads leading out north and south from here." The artist Henry Miller in 1855 reported finding "part of a human skeleton bound to a tree; part of the bones had fallen to the ground, the flesh had all gone and only some dried skin was remaining. The skull laid [*sic*] on the ground, cleft in two towards the left skull."

The towns were even worse than the countryside. Gangs of thugs for a few years practically controlled San Francisco, whose population by the end of 1849 had increased by eighty thousand. Many ex-convicts from Australia found a criminal home in San Francisco, where they were known as the Sydney Ducks and engaged in gambling, arson and extortion. Irish from the slums of New York, where they had earned a fearsome reputation in gangs like the Bowery Boys, had enlisted in the New York Regiment during the Mexican War. *The Annals of San Francisco* observed that the "most noted blackguards of the country" came from the New York Regiment. After their discharge or desertion, many banded together into a gang in San Francisco and called themselves the Hounds, and later the Regulators. Their headquarters was a tent they called Tammany Hall. The Hounds liked to parade through the streets to music by day and terrorize Latin Americans by night. One favorite diversion was to enter a bar or restaurant en masse, eat and drink extravagantly, and then before leaving demolish the furniture

Throughout the state, civil authority both executive and legislative was thoroughly corrupted by cronyism and bribery. Political quarrels frequently erupted into full-scale riots, and enemies often settled their differences with duels, the number of which, according to *The Annals of San Francisco,* was "fearfully great." Newspaper editors could be murdered for their opinions, like Edward Gilbert of the *Alta California,* who in 1852 was killed in a duel over an article accusing one of Governor Bigler's cronies of profiting from legislation passed to aid overland immigrants. One Sacramento newspaper described the political leaders of the 1850s as "that delectable crowd of brandy-drinking, pistol-shooting, swearing, swaggering gentry who turn up their noses at all honest work." In 1852 the *Alta California* editorialized against the "official rottenness and degradation," which held the people "spell bound, and enchained by the potency of a corrupt press." San Francisco particularly was "a hotbed of political corruption and infamy."

And there were numerous gangs of Mexican and Californio bandits, led by chieftains like Salomon Pico, Claudio Feliz, Pio Linares, Juan Flores, Joaquín Valenzuela and of course Joaquín Murieta, who preyed upon travelers, immigrants, cattle buyers, *rancheros* and miners throughout California from Bodega Bay to San Diego. Pio Linares, a cousin of the former governor Pio Pico, and his Irish companion the gambler Jack Powers, were notorious cattle thieves in the San Luis Obispo area with a sideline on those traveling the El Camino Real. The horrific skeleton discovered by Henry Miller was probably one of their unfortunate victims.

The upshot was a murder rate unmatched in American history. Los Angeles was particularly violent. According to a Los Angeles weekly of the early 1850s, four deaths in one week made "a poor week for killing." In Los Angeles between July of 1850 and October of 1851 some 44 people were murdered out of a population of 8,500—which translates to a murder rate of 414 out of 100,000. (By way of comparison, Los Angeles in 1998 had a murder rate of nearly 12 per

100,000; in Washington, D.C., the most violent city in America, the rate was nearly 50 per 100,000.) The same high rate of murder holds true for the northern counties in the late 1840s and early 1850s. Nor was this rate of violence typical of America in the nineteenth century: for most of that century both Philadelphia and Boston posted murder rates of about 3 per 100,000.

The level of violence and the absence of civil institutions, particularly in the mining regions, led to vigilantism. In 1851, after the brutal murder of a merchant, the citizens of San Francisco formed the secret Committee of Vigilance, which eventually grew to eight thousand members. Elsewhere, impromptu lynchings administered justice when the government and police were incapable of controlling crime, and more than two hundred malefactors, real and alleged, were hanged between 1849 and 1853. By the late fifties civic and governmental institutions were in place for punishing criminals, and vigilantism, arguably necessary in the disorderly years between the Gold Rush and statehood, degenerated into mob mayhem, often directed against innocent Mexicans and other Hispanics.

The criminal career of Joaquín Murieta and the actions taken to hunt him down must be understood in this context of predatory violence and swift retribution. The paradigm of race and oppression—Hispanic bandits taking retributive action against the Anglo interlopers who stole their land—does not adequately answer to the historical reality.

It is true that some Californios, angered by the ignorant nativism and arrogance of recent Yankee immigrants, covertly or openly sympathized with and aided the Mexican bandits, and a few became bandits themselves—men like Pio Linares, the son of a Californio judge in San Luis Obispo. Linares preyed on immigrants traveling the El Camino Real and in 1858 died in a fierce gun-battle with a posse. Looking back on that period in 1875, Mariano Vallejo wrote that "most of the young who had been so unjustly despoiled, thirsty for vengeance, filled the ranks of Joaquín Murieta, and under his leadership were able to revenge some of the insults that the North American people had inflicted on them." Vallejo, though, may have been projecting his own bitterness—when he wrote these words his vast properties and fortune had been lost—back onto a time when the Californio elite could not yet be described as "despoiled."

But the Californio sympathy for Mexican bandits perhaps reflected not so much racial solidarity as the old principle that the enemy of my enemy is my friend. Californios generally despised Mexicans and Sonorans, and were not above exploiting them for profit. Jesus Luna, justice of the peace for San Luis Obispo, owned a café and dancehall right on the El Camino Real. The droves of immigrant Mexicans had to pass down this road on their way to the gold mines in the north. Luna charged them fifty cents a head before he let them leave town. One of his enforcers was Pio Linares—and the posse that pursued Linares was headed by the Californio Francisco Castro, sheriff of San Luis Obispo County.

In fact, Californios and their cattle herds were often the victims of bandits, and Californios frequently participated in bringing them to justice. The story of the crimes and capture of one the most notorious gangs in Los Angeles County illustrates how simplistic notions of racial solidarity break down when one considers the facts of what daily life was actually like. Juan Flores was a Californio who in 1857 hooked up with one Pancho Daniel, an alleged veteran of Joaquín Murieta's gang and reputed slayer of forty men. Along with thirteen other bandits, they murdered a German storekeeper in San Juan Capistrano. A posse of five men lead by Sheriff James Barton happened upon the gang, and there ensued a bloody shootout that left several bandits wounded and Sheriff Barton and three other possemen dead.

Although the bandits were Californios and Mexicans and the possemen were Yankees, the "respectable," i.e. affluent, Californios of Los Angeles demanded action. The Spanish-language newspaper *El Clamor Publico* reminded Californios that their "society is linked with indissoluble bonds to that of the Americans." They should "lay aside all animosity" and prove their loyalty by helping track down the killers. Apparently many Californios agreed, for one of the leaders of the manhunt was Andres Pico, brother of Alta California's last Mexican governor and a hero of the Battle of San Pascual (he subsequently became a state senator). He was accompanied by another veteran of that battle, Tomas Sanchez, who became sheriff of Los

Angeles County. The posses were also helped by Indians who guarded the mountain passes.

After a long pursuit, several gun-battles, daring escapes by some of the bandits and summary executions of others, Flores was captured and ultimately hanged by a vigilante mob. Earlier Pico himself had hanged two of the bandits and cut off their ears, perhaps sending a message to his bandit cousin Salomon Pico, who reportedly collected the ears of his victims. Pancho Daniel managed to delay his trial by using the services of an able Anglo lawyer, but to no avail; a mob got to him too, and he was hanged. According to the *Los Angeles Star,* there was "nothing to indicate that the respectable portion of the Californians were dissatisfied with the result." Yet there were troubling racial dimensions to the pursuit and execution of the outlaws: innocent Hispanics were caught up in the hysteria and hanged along with the murderers—the vigilantes killed twelve men, not counting Daniel, only four of whom were members of the Flores-Daniel gang.

One of the worst examples of early "racial profiling" occurred after the Rancheria Massacre of 1855. Nine bandits, including a red-headed American, after robbing some Chinese rode into the Gold Rush mining town of Rancheria and shot up a hotel, leaving six people dead, including an Indian and the hotel keeper's wife. An enraged mob began rounding up every Mexican in sight. Thirty-six were marched to the hanging tree, but only three of them, falsely identified as part of the gang, were lynched. Run out of town, the Mexicans fled to a nearby ravine, where Indians, angry over the Indian victim, killed at least eight more. The exact number is uncertain since some of the victims were devoured by hogs. Another suspect was hanged in Gopher Flat, and the mob drove the Mexicans from the camp. Chile Flat in Drytown was burned to the ground, including the Catholic Church. A posse eventually hunted down the real bandits, who managed to kill a few more lawmen before being shot down or captured and hanged. Twenty-three people died altogether.

But race is only part of the story; respectability and social status were important defining categories as well. When Abel Stearns gave a ball in honor of George Washington in 1852, he invited the "best" Californios but snubbed the Yankee gamblers. When the latter tried to crash the party, Andres Pico picked off two of them from a window. And as Leonard Pitt observes, "Mexicans were nearly as alienated from Californios as Californios were from Yankees." No matter how much Californios resented the boorish nativism and anti-Catholic prejudices of Anglo newcomers, those among them who were landowning and "respectable," particularly in the south where they were more numerous and influential, found some measure of solidarity with their fellow *ricos* (rich men) and property owners no matter what their origins. These were the men with whom they forged the ruling class: in the early years of statehood, Pitt notes, Californios at one time or another "obtained practically every imaginable public office," from sheriff and justice of the peace to mayor and state senator.

SEVEN

The ethnic variety and intricate racial interrelations of Californians have always eluded explanation by reductionist melodramas based on race. Our contemporary identity politics has essentialized a stereotypical racial identity that often distorts a more fluid and quirky human reality. Spanish colonial societies did define persons by racial heritage, with fifty-six categories (*castas*) ranged on a scale from darker to lighter, with a corresponding increase in social status the lighter one got. But these categories were not irrevocably fixed. "White" usually signified pure Spanish blood, but could also include those of mixed blood. Thus, as historian Lisbeth Haas says, "Race categories remained relatively flexible concepts, constituting, on the frontier, one of but a number of attributes that defined status (others included religion, wealth, and legitimate birth)." Speaking Spanish and practicing Catholicism marked one as a *gente de razón,* a "person with reason," as opposed to the savage Indian *sin razón.* Thus even those with Indian blood could consider themselves "white," although a high premium was placed on Spanish blood. Ignacio Sepúlveda, a judge in Los Angeles whose family once owned what is now Santa Monica and Venice, in 1874 wrote, "There are [a] great many families in whose veins circulates much of the *sangre azul* [blue blood] of Spain."

The regional identity of the Californios was often also expressed in terms of physical difference from the inhabitants of Mexico.

Sepúlveda asserted that Californios "differ in many essential particulars from the other people of Mexico," including "traits of character, features, and mental gifts." Comments by Anglo visitors to California both support and contradict this assertion of physical difference. Bayard Taylor wrote that "the Californians, as a race, are vastly superior to the Mexicans. They have larger frames, stronger muscles, and a fresh, ruddy complexion." A Californio informed Taylor that because of those physical distinctions, Californio soldiers were dubbed "Americanos" by the Mexicans. In 1854 *The Annals of San Francisco* prefaced a catalogue of insulting stereotypes about Mexicans by noting, "It is not of . . . the native Californians, who are gentlemen by nature, that we speak." Yet a few years earlier Richard Henry Dana had dismissed Californios as "lazy half-breeds." The contradiction is perhaps explained by the fact that Californios included both Spanish and mixed-blood, with the former dominating the upper classes.

The intermarriage of Yankee and British settlers with the wealthier Californios also blurred racial categories and favored money and respectability as markers of status. The influx of Mexicans that attended the Gold Rush complicated the picture even further. A mixed-blood Californio might look down on a *mestizo* from Sonora, whom he called *calzonero blanco* or "white trousers" for his billowy white pants, and at the same time be lumped in with him by unconversant Yankees who knew nothing of these subtle differences between native Californios and more recent Mexican arrivals. So too, American newcomers indiscriminately categorized the Californio (or Chilean or Peruvian immigrant) of pure Spanish blood as a "greaser." Hispanics returned the favor and called all Americans and Europeans *gringos,* a word perhaps derived from *griego,* "Greek," a term used of any foreigner that also could mean "gibberish." Every group had a nickname: a German was called "Dutch," a corruption of "Deutsch," and Frenchmen "keskydees," which is what an American heard when a Frenchman asked, "Qu'est-ce qu'il dit?" ("What did he say?").

The collision between a fixed and a more fluid concept of race became clear in the Constitutional Convention of 1849. Of the Californio delegates, only one was of mixed blood. Nonetheless, the limitation of voting rights to "white males" disturbed the Californios.

As Pablo de la Guerra informed the conventioneers, "[M]any citizens of California have received from nature a very dark skin; nevertheless, there are among them men who have hitherto been allowed to vote, and not only that, but to fill the highest public offices." Again, "whiteness" meant in effect being respectable, practicing Catholicism and speaking Spanish, with the proviso of not being pure Indian or black. Another Californio delegate agreed with this last qualification: "If by the word 'white' it was intended to exclude the African race, then it was correct and satisfactory." The outcome in any case was that the more uncompromising view of race prevailed, and in 1857 the *mestizo* delegate Manuel Dominguez was barred by law from testifying in a trial.

The Gold Rush greatly widened the ethnic spectrum, as we saw earlier: by 1852 there were sixty thousand foreigners in California, and newspapers were published in French, German, Spanish, Italian and Chinese. A visitor to a bull-and-bear fight commented on the men of "all sizes, colors, and classes such as California, and California alone, can bring together." Such a medley gave wide scope for indulging in the ethnic stereotyping prevalent at the time. *The Annals of San Francisco* wrote of Germans and French, "The true Germans dote on *lager beer* and they are a heavy, phlegmatic, unambitious race; the French love wines and they are as sparkling yet without strength or force of character." The Anglo-Saxon, however, "is a giant when he begins to work, tearing and trampling over the *impossibilities* of other races and binding them to his absolute, insolent will."

Chauvinism on the part of Americans had ample opportunity to show itself in the hothouse of economic competition. Large numbers of war veterans in the gold fields only served to worsen race relations, as these old soldiers continued to see the Mexican miners as foes and interlopers. But not all Americans approved of such prejudiced attitudes. In 1850 the *Stockton Times* satirized the racist mentality in the character of "Jack Rowdy," who boasts, "Mexicans have no business in this country. I don't believe in them. The men were made to be shot at.... An American is justifiable in shooting every foreigner that disputes his whim." And a few years later the *Alta California* condemned the "disgraceful acts" and "intolerant and mobbish proceedings" directed by Anglo miners, "reckless plundering men" who "call themselves Americans," against foreign immigrants who were defended as "respectable, intelligent and industrious." But such voices were overwhelmed by the sheer numbers of gold-hungry argonauts who saw Mexicans as the despised competition, and a recently conquered people to boot.

Yet ethnic cooperation existed as well, racial boundaries yielding to commonly shared concerns. The slave Stephen Spencer Hill, who had come to California from Arkansas with his master, bought his freedom in 1853 and started up a farming business. His former master sent a friend named Rozier to reclaim him. Hill's white neighbors took up a collection, hired lawyers, harvested his crops and hid his valuables so they couldn't be seized. Failing to prove his freedom, Hill escaped to Stockton with Rozier's watch and a draft for $500. Neighbors who were threatened by marauding Indians could also work cooperatively. An expedition in the winter of 1850–51 against some stock-stealing Miwoks comprised fifty Americans, twenty-five Mexicans and seventy-five French veterans of the *Garde mobile.* The latter had been used to put down rioters in Paris during the revolution of 1848 but then became an embarrassment to the French authorities, who packed them off to California.

We have noted how criminal gangs, their victims and the posses formed to hound them down were ethnically mixed—like the posse that tracked, tried and executed the mixed band responsible for the San Miguel massacre, or the one that captured Pio Linares. Outlaws, even those regarded as ethnic heroes, were not averse to riding with *gringos:* Pio Linares numbered among his associates Jack Powers, the notorious Irish gambler and desperado who escaped prosecution for his crimes in California, only to be murdered by *vaqueros* on his Arizona ranch, his body cast to the hogs; the brigand Salomon Pico, another putative relative of Andres Pico, teamed up with the horse thief William Otis Hall; and Pancho Daniel rode with Thomas King. Race is of course vital in the story of early California, but so are the many other ways men experience solidarity and conflict. In the bubbling caldron that was Gold Rush California, ethnic identity and loyalties were shifting and fluid indeed.

EIGHT

The meteoric career of Joaquín Murieta lasted only a few years, from about 1850 to 1853, but it ran concurrently with the most intense phase of social disruption. Alonzo Delano wrote that in 1850 two hundred people had been murdered, but only one murderer had been legally executed. California, he complained, had degenerated into a state "which bordered on anarchy and threatened to dissolve the social compact of the community."

Much of this crime and mayhem was committed by disaffected Californios and Mexicans who formed shifting bands of outlaws that preyed with impunity on anyone possessing property. Some of these men, as we have seen, were mere predators, though the insults and injuries they may have suffered at the hands of Americans no doubt added the spice of revenge to crimes whose motives were mercenary. These outlaws may have had what they perceived to be valid reasons for attacking society in an attempt to redress injustices, and perhaps defended their crimes by calling themselves *insurrectos,* rebels against the new American order.

Yes, Californio bandits could plausibly have considered themselves revolutionaries fighting Anglo domination, but there is little direct evidence that any did so. After the Flores-Daniel incident described above, people began to speak of the "Flores revolution," but given that prominent Californios participated in capturing the criminals, one wonders on whose behalf the "revolution" was being waged, and how indiscriminate murder and robbery, particularly against unthreatening Chinese newcomers, were supposed to advance it. As historian John Boessenecker writes of the Flores-Daniel gang, "The murder of an inoffensive shopkeeper, a popular sheriff, and three well-liked possemen was beyond the pale, and many Californios did not hesitate to join the manhunt, even while the poorest of Californios and Mexican peons may have admired the exploits of the Hispanic bandits." The evidence suggests that rather than being revolutionaries, these men were criminal opportunists who took advantage of an unsettled society awash in gold and livestock.

Mexican immigrants like Joaquín Murieta, moreover, had little historical basis for considering themselves revolutionaries. They had come to California, now a United States territory, for the gold, which they could obtain by mining or by means of robbery; and for horses, whether mustangs rounded up in the San Joaquin Valley or branded horses stolen from *rancheros.* Californios developed a distinct identity and tended to be condescending towards Mexico; indeed what they resented, more than any Anglo mistreatment of Mexicans, was the indiscriminate way they and the Mexicans were lumped together. So there is no reason to think that Mexican immigrants would feel so much solidarity with Californios that they would throw in their lot with them in rebellion. After all, they had shown little interest in the region before the Mexican War.

But Mexicans and Californios did share one just cause for resentment against Anglos—the short-lived Foreign Miners Tax.

Passed in April of 1850, this law taxed foreign miners by requiring them to buy a license for $20 a month. The purpose of the law, according to its legislative sponsor, Colonel Thomas Jefferson Green—an adventurer from Texas about whom Sam Houston once remarked, "He has all the characteristics of a dog except fidelity"—was to stem the tide of immigration, "a vast multitude ... of the worst population of the Mexican and South American states, New South Wales, and the Southern Islands [Hawaii]." The governor of each county appointed tax collectors who were allowed to keep three of the twenty dollars they collected for the license. Anyone who resisted payment could have his claim taken from him by somebody else. American miners were only too happy to accompany the tax collector and employ violence against those who were unwilling to pay, particularly in the southern mines where most of the Sonorans were mining. Hundreds packed up and left.

Although the more numerous Mexicans bore the brunt of the tax, other foreigners were targeted as well—once more, greed more than race was the dynamic. Californio Antonio Franco Coronel in his memoirs listed four reasons for the Yankee miners' dislike of the Mexicans, none of which includes racial prejudice: the Sonorans were more successful, the Californios were there first, the American immigrants were low-class ruffians, and finally the "terrible fever to obtain gold."

Incidents of organized resistance to the tax illustrate the multiethnic makeup of the targeted miners. When Lorenzo A. Besançon went to Tuolumne County to collect the tax, a coalition of Mexican, Chilean and French miners gathered together, the latter so numerous that one observer called the affair the "French Revolution." The protesters made camp at American Camp and sent delegates to the governor with a petition protesting the tax. Anglos, incited by rumors of incendiary speeches calling for armed resistance, marched into the camp as, in the description of Benjamin Harris, "the foreigners, with streamers, banners, and flags, were parading the streets . . . preceded by a naked Indian daubed in war paint, all singing the *Marseillaise* and other Revolutionary Songs." Another gathering reportedly consisted of Alsatians and Basques; and still another group at Murphy's Camp, which was made up of French, German and Spanish-speaking miners, marched to Sonora, including in their number one Madame Louis dressed in pantaloons, a revolutionary-red shirt and a sombrero.

Rather than resist, many foreign miners simply left, the Mexicans back to Mexico, the French to San Francisco. Others apparently engaged in acts of retaliation. The increasing disorder stirred the flames of prejudice and vigilantism. Meetings of Anglo miners passed resolutions against presumably criminal foreigners, including "Peons of Mexico," "renegades of South America," and the "convicts of the British Empire," meaning the Australians. Perhaps as many as fifteen thousand Mexicans left the southern diggings.

Clearly, racial prejudice played a part in the expulsion of Mexican miners, but other factors were important as well. Some Latin Americans, and Californios as well, worked their claims with Indian labor, which struck some Americans as virtual slavery. Southern Americans who tried to mine with slaves were unwelcome as well. Theodore Johnson recalled meeting in the southern diggings "a large party of Peruvians and Chilians [*sic*], with their Indian *peones* or slaves." In 1849 a meeting of Anglo miners on the Tuolumne River issued a proclamation protesting the "appearance among us of influential men from distant provinces of Mexico, Peru, Chile, the Sandwich Islands & etc., with large bands of hired men, who are nominally slaves." The miners demanded that "all classes of slaves or hired serfs coming from distant countries" be expelled. Obviously, fear of competition rather than concern for the oppressed "peons" was the miners' principal motivation, but also at work was a perceived cultural contrast between Anglo Protestantism, with its veneration of free labor, and Hispanic quasi-feudal practices.

Some Anglo miners even protested the intimidation and use of force that frequently accompanied the collection of the tax, understandably resisted by many miners, who barely averaged $20 a month after expenses and were not happy about being driven from their claims. One miners' meeting passed a resolution that disapproved of "any act of violence committed against peaceable persons of any race." An editorial in the *Daily Alta California* in San Francisco, protesting against the nativist prejudice that lay behind the tax, cried, "Shame! Shame! To spit on a man because he was born under a warmer sun than shone upon our birth." Merchants particularly disliked the tax, as it drove away business, since many foreign miners, especially Mexicans who were relatively close to their homes in Mexico, spent their gold on merchandise, not to mention the vast sums spent drinking and gambling. Merchant William Perkins called the tax "illegal, unjust, abortive and extremely prejudicial to the best interests of the state." So too the editors of the *Stockton Times,* who noted the "ruinous effect" of the tax upon the merchants as well as the "universal feeling of distrust among the miners." By 1851 the tax was repealed, to be revived a few years later after the influx of Chinese once more threatened Anglo miners with too much competition.

The Foreign Miners Tax forms the background to an important element of the Murieta myth, the abuse the bandit allegedly received at the hands of Anglo miners when he attempted to work his claim. So too does another piece of legislation, the California Land Act of 1851, one more charge in the indictment of American dispossession of the Californios.

NINE

When the myriad immigrants from the United States became familiar with the estates of the Californio ranchers, they encountered a culture of ownership and land use that was utterly foreign to their tradition of yeomen working their own farms. On the most general level, the controversy that followed reflected the ancient conflict between the herdsman and the farmer, the former dominating wide areas of seldom improved land, the latter hungering for soil that could be intensively cultivated—the very theme, of course, of numerous Western legends. An editorial in a Sacramento newspaper in 1852 claimed divine sanction for the law "that the earth shall be occupied by those who understand and appropriate it to its intended uses.... Those who will not use the earth, will not be permitted to cumber it." Likewise the homesteading mentality, enshrined in law, preferred legitimate acquisition of public lands by those who would improve them, at a cost of $1.25 per acre up to 160 acres. Many settlers did not care to wait for a government survey to distinguish between public land that could be legitimately homesteaded, from the sprawling, vaguely marked estates of the *rancheros.*

Moreover, ignorant of or indifferent to the Treaty of Guadalupe Hidalgo, which guaranteed the former citizens of Mexico their land rights, the newcomers saw instead a handful of conquered people dominating huge expanses of land in a country that now belonged to the United States, land that in their view was being wasted. History shows us that farmers seldom are content to let mounted warriors monopolize good land. John Keegan's comments regarding the opening of the Great Plains to settlers once the Sioux had been defeated are pertinent here: "[The] claim ... of less than a million people, to possess territories capable of supporting not only millions more directly settled, but of still more millions outside America waiting to be fed by those territories' product, is the claim not of oppressed primitives but of the selfish rich." This stricture applies with even more justice to the big California *rancheros,* whose territories, worked by serf-like Indians, went to support a lifestyle of pure consumption, status and display more typical of an aristocracy than a democracy.

To say all this, however, is not to imply that those who squatted on Californio land were all salt-of-the-earth pioneers like the Starret family in the film *Shane.* High levels of demand from hungry miners and the shortage of food meant that a few seasons of farming could be highly profitable; and as historian J. S. Holliday writes, "The farmers in the 1850s pursued profits with no less avidity than the miners and merchants." Two farmers near San Jose grossed $150,000 in one year on 130 acres of potatoes, onion, tomatoes and cabbages. The high demand for wheat and barley also made the extensive, flat grasslands of some *ranchos* attractive. A couple of harvests from someone else's land could earn a squatter enough money to buy his own land or finance a mining expedition.

Many Americans, then, simply squatted on *ranchero* land and began working it—in 1854, about 1,500 people squatted on one grant. In 1850 the city of Oakland was laid out on the Rancho San Antonio owned by the Peralta family. Turmoil and violence followed the squatters, as "land pirates" burned crops, killed livestock, harassed and sometimes killed *vaqueros* and *rancheros,* threatened judges and attacked surveyors. In 1853 the *Alta California* protested that "old rancheros have been completely stripped of all their possessions, the squatter not leaving them even their gardens, orchards, or goods," their herds driven off to be slaughtered or sold. Legal shenanigans—bribery, nuisance suits and forged documents—tormented the *rancheros* as well. California was riven by these opposing interests, and demands for a solution resulted first in two reports to the United States government, and then the 1851 bill.

One of the problems noted in the first report, done by Captain Henry Halleck, soon to find fame as a general in the Civil War, was the casual way the boundaries of grants were described. Most grants frequently contained the phrase *mas o menos,* "more or less," and boundaries were sometimes defined by markers such as the following, from the Rancho San Antonio that became Oakland: the boundary stretched from the "bullock's skull" to the "fork in the cow path" to the "sycamore" to the "hatchet-blazed stump." Another grant's southern limit was described as "the place where Don Simeon Castro sits on his white horse each evening." Halleck found as well that many grants never complied with the terms of their original concession, such as the requirement to provide a map, and many were tainted with fraud and other irregularities. Given that homesteaders had a right to improve public lands, these ill-defined boundaries made it difficult if not impossible to know which lands were which—not that squatters always cared.

The California Land Act attempted to sort out these various conflicts. It called for a board of three commissioners who would examine all titles held under Spanish and Mexican grants. The commission began its work in December of 1851 and heard cases for five years. During that time it examined 800 grants covering 12 million acres; 520 claims were approved, 273 rejected and the remainder were either dismissed by the commission or withdrawn. Decisions could be appealed to the federal courts, and of 132 claimants who made appeals, 98 won reversal of the commission's decision. About 90 cases were taken to the United States Supreme Court, where again most decisions favored the claimants.

What ruined the *rancheros* was not an American government bent on dispossessing them of land in order to give it to Yankee squatters; rather it was the process itself, which was difficult and expensive—claims took on average seventeen years before they were decided. Many Californios were ignorant of American law and frequently did not speak English. Lost documents and nebulous boundaries made it difficult to establish grants or prove their validity. *Rancheros* thus were dependent on sometimes unscrupulous and exorbitant lawyers, who charged fees anywhere from one-fourth to two-fifths of the land's value. Many lawyers ended up owning the land in lieu of payment; when he left California in 1857, William Tecumseh Sherman said, "I have no respect for the Law and the Lawyers here." And all the while the depredations and political agitation of the squatters assailed the *rancheros,* many of whom ended up ruined. The Peralta family's Rancho San Antonio—now the site of Oakland, Alameda and Berkeley—was sold off bit by bit at bargain prices as the owners fought the squatters who pitched tents in their pastures and the land agents who challenged the deeds and inheritances. By the time title was confirmed in 1885, most of the land was gone. The Peralta family's experience was typical of most Californio *rancheros:* as early as 1870, seven-eighths of the land was owned by European immigrants and Americans.

The racialist interpretation of the land controversy, however, in which colluding Yankees finish the job of stealing California from its rightful owners, obscures a complex reality. Many landowners, including prominent men such as Hugo Reid and John Marsh, were English or American, and had to prove their titles as well. John C. Frémont, by then a California senator, opposed the bill, as title to his own 44,000-acre Rancho Mariposas would have to be validated. John Sutter took his case all the way to the United States Supreme Court, and though eventually he had title confirmed, the lengthy and expensive process broke him. Rather than being the tool of their interests, the commission was believed by squatters to favor the *rancheros,* and the state government was not always sympathetic to their demands. A law requiring landowners to pay for "improvements" by trespassing squatters was overturned by the supreme court, and another that would have allowed a squatter to occupy eighty acres of a disputed grant never passed.

Nor were *rancheros* the only victims of the squatters. Americans in San Francisco and Sacramento who purchased land from Mexican grantees found their property appropriated by squatters who did not recognize the original grant and so felt justified in disregarding the sale. These claims were frequently backed with violence and vandalism. In Sacramento, squatters organized into a Settlers Association that in 1850 got into a gunfight with the mayor and a posse trying to evict them. The mayor was shot four times, but survived only to die of cholera the next year.

Yet in the end, the ruling aristocracy of California was nearly obliterated, its influence in California finished. Droughts, competition from new breeds of cattle and herds driven from Texas, the burdens of establishing land titles and the eventual political and economic dominance of the farmers, all fatally weakened the *rancheros.* The culprit was not just racism, though ethnic prejudices fueled the rhetoric, but the old, relentless human demand for land to feed and house an exploding population. The Californio *ranchero,* like the mounted knight of Romance, was a doomed anachronism fated to live on only in legend.

TEN

The historical events sketched above were concentrated in a period of a few years. Their underlying patterns, in all their dramatic intensity, are manifested in the career of Murieta, which perhaps helps explain why of all the many badmen of that time, the shadowy "Joaquín," the shootout at Cantua Creek and the bottled head seized the imagination of Californians.

As we shall see, perennial folk themes and oral tales would keep the myth alive too. The wronged man who uses violence to avenge injustice is an archetype as old as Homer's Achilles. And the folk figure of the outlaw became increasingly popular near the century's turn, as the disappearing frontier became the stuff of dime novels and lurid serials. Local pride also contributed to Murieta's popularity, particularly for those Gold Rush communities that, once the gold was gone, had only their imagined folk history, of the sort made famous by Bret Harte's sentimental stories, to provide civic esteem and remind them of lost glory.

But the history of these critical years reveals more important forces that would resonate through the decades and make Murieta a compelling symbol beyond the gold country and California. The collision of cultures, with its attendant complexities of race, was sparked by the Mexican War but exploded in the Gold Rush, accelerating a process of change already begun in California when the Yankee merchants and tradesmen began settling there. In the figure of Murieta—a dashing and daring horseman who attacked the perceived agents of that change—Californios and later immigrants from Mexico found a powerful symbol of their own disappointments and injustices and lost grandeur. That the haughty Californio in fact looked down on such desperados and frequently had been their victim were realities soon forgotten in the face of American economic, political and cultural dominance.

Finally, the carnage of those years, the violence both of criminals and vigilantes, speaks to a permanent human fascination with the drama of death, a drama compellingly embodied in the deeds and the beheading of Murieta. At some primal level that we frequently avoid acknowledging, people admire the killer, whether outlaw or vigilante, and the brutal simplicity with which he resolves conflict. For most people, even in America of the nineteenth century, such slaughter was rare and usually encountered only in imaginary form; stable social institutions existed to police and punish it. But in California of the late 1840s and early 1850s, when civic and social order was rudimentary at best, abrupt and savage bloodletting was a daily reality. Murieta and his bottled head catered to that fascination for early Californians, and once transformed into myth and legend continued to stir the imaginations of people far beyond California and long after the Gold Rush.

Myth

The uncertainty surrounding the identities of the bandits terrorizing California; the confusion over which Joaquín was *the* Joaquín; the conflicting reports about the gunfight at Cantua Creek; the questions about which Rangers actually took part in the fight, and the continuing doubts about exactly whose head was being put on show—all created near-perfect conditions for the invention of a myth. Even before John Rollin Ridge created the most influential version of the Joaquín legend in his novel *The Life and Adventures of Joaquín Murieta,* which came out a year after the climactic shootout, the lack of factual information about him was being made good by the fabrications of newspapers.

ONE

An important early newspaper account established some critical details of what would become the Murieta legend. The *Sacramento Daily Union* of February 14, 1853, and the *San Joaquin Republican* two days later, both republished a story that had appeared probably February 13 in the *San Francisco Whig and Advertiser.* The correspondent claimed to have heard the story from "an intelligent Mexican who resided in the city of Mexico during the invasion of General Scott" and who supposedly had known Murieta. This habit of publishing second- and third-hand accounts from shadowy "correspondents," along with the Victorian newspapers' penchant for moralizing, makes it very hard to separate factual details from journalistic fiction.

In this version of Joaquín's life, the bandit was born in Villa de Catorce in the state of Jalisco and is thirty-five years old. His disposition "cruel and sanguinary," he is one of the "most crafty and daring guerillas of Mexico," a onetime member of the guerilla band of the famous Padre Jaranta. (Fr. Caledonio Domeco Jaranta was a guerilla leader who harassed the American forces occupying Mexico City until he was killed in 1848.) Six feet tall and of "immense muscular strength ... [with a] dark, sallow complexion," Joaquín is "chief of a notorious band of robbers now infesting the vicinity of Mexico" while living in California. Their specialty is preying on Mexicans traveling from Mexico to California, according to the *Republican,* whereas the *Union* notes that his band is "sufficiently numerous to pillage and destroy in ranches and thinly inhabited portions of the mines." He is "known to wear a coat of armor," and when shot at "receives the ball on his breast with perfect indifference." In Mexico, Joaquín travels freely in the disguise of a friar, aided by his influence with the Mexican soldiery. Mexicans "look upon him as a brave man, and he is considered a person of some education."

These newspaper stories reveal how the persona of Murieta was being constructed out of both the anxieties of Americans and their mythic longings. Particularly revealing is the assertion that Joaquín at one time was a guerilla fighting American forces. Later in August the *Alta California* would report that Murieta's cruel sidekick, "Four-Fingered Jack," had spent time in Mexico helping to raise an army to retake California. This identification of the bandits with the Mexican guerillas resisting the invading American army tapped into powerful fears and resentments among Americans who had fought in the Mexican War or who had merely read about the guerillas' activities. One particularly gruesome and widely reported episode occurred in February 1847. Guerillas along with mounted lancers attacked a United States Army supply train on its way to Monterey in Mexico. Nearly all the American teamsters and soldiers were slaughtered or burned in their wagons, and their bodies were mutilated. In revenge, some American troops attacked a nearby village and killed as many as forty peasants. This vicious circle of revenge was an important feature of American-Mexican relations, and it is no surprise that Joaquín would be plugged into this already familiar pattern.

This motif of Joaquín as a resister against Yankee tyranny recurs over and over, perhaps speaking to Americans' ambivalence about their occupation of California and their relationship to Mexico. More probably, the linkage of Murieta to Mexican resistance was a device for convincing citizens of the seriousness of Mexican banditry by giving it a political dimension and connecting it to a potential violent overthrow of American rule. And imagining an organized guerilla band with sympathizers among the Californios explained how Joaquín could commit so many crimes and still elude capture.

Baser motives were at work as well. Harry Love, who was made the captain of the California Rangers that tracked the bandits, after the gunfight at Cantua Creek set about spreading tales about armed guerilla bands, no doubt in an attempt to extend the Rangers' commission, which was set to expire mid-August 1853. In an interview with the *Republican* on August 11, Love warned of the "bands of Mexican guerillas which infest the country" from Sonora to Shasta, especially in the Coast Range, which hides "hordes of desperate villains." Joaquín, Love asserted, could quickly raise two thousand desperadoes in order "to scour the entire southern country, sack the small settlements, and ... announce himself at Sonora," presumably as the prelude to the recovery of Alta California for Mexico. This disaster is imminent "unless effective measures be taken," such measures to include, of course, insuring that the Rangers "be left in the field" under the command of Captain Love.

Other details from the newspaper stories—Joaquín's craftiness, his bravery, even his "armor" ("to what base use has the armor of the days of chivalry come," the *Calaveras Chronicle* complained)—all contribute to another important persona the bandit manifested: the spirited, debonair figure of Romance and adventure. Already two enduring components of the Murieta myth, political resistance and Romance, are in place in these first accounts.

Between these stories and another important one that appeared in April 1853, the newspapers continued to add hearsay details. He had "presided over a monte table" in the gold country, his gang was well organized all the way to Shasta, and he had once been "principal *vaquero* for Dr. Marsh," one of northern California's early pioneers. The need to link well-known public figures to one another, apparently a widespread folklore motif, will surface repeatedly in later versions of the Murieta myth. Earlier reports that Americans were riding with Joaquín are repeated: "There is no doubt," the *Republican* reported, "that some white men, whose names are yet unknown, are privy to the acts of the marauders." This belief undoubtedly reflected the fact that many bandits were white, and no doubt identified themselves as Joaquín or as part of his gang in order to cover their tracks. Racial one-upmanship also helps to explain this belief: Joaquín, the *Republican* wrote, "must be aided by white men in his nefarious proceedings" since he is "a poor, miserable, cowardly Mexican."

On April 18 a lengthy story appeared in the *San Francisco Herald* that further fixed and elaborated on the Romantic aspect of Joaquín. The newspaper said the story came from an unnamed "Monterey correspondent" who had heard it from a *ranchero* living on the Salinas plains near Monterey. One night the *ranchero* was visited by a man who "civilly" asked for food, claiming to be heading south to purchase cattle. He was "armed to the teeth," a "tall handsome man, about 21 years old, with a long beard, and apparently false moustache, and [he] carried four revolvers and a large bowie knife." He announced to the *ranchero,* "Sir, I am that Joaquin, and no man takes me alive, or comes within one hundred yards of me with these good weapons." The announcement "I am Joaquín" will become a signature to many versions of the legend.

Joaquín then told his story: he had been "oppressed, robbed, and persecuted by the Americans in the placers [mines] ... insulted and grossly maltreated without justice—had been flogged—and he was determined to be revenged for his wrongs four-fold." Joaquín is bitterly disillusioned about Americans, having once been "a great admirer" of what he thought were "the most generous, noble, and liberal people in the world ... to whom tyrany [*sic*] and injustice were ... hateful." He had migrated to California, "thinking to end my days in California as a citizen of the United States." But in every activity he pursued he was "swindled and robbed" by "the very men for whom I had had the greatest friendship and admiration." At last he vowed, "I will revenge my wrongs, and take the law into my own hands; those who injured me I'll slay, and those who have not, I'll rob—my track shall leave a trail of blood, and he that seeks me shall bite the dust, or I will die in the struggle." The bandit then left, but not before paying the *ranchero* for his hospitality.

This tale establishes a perennial component of the myth: Joaquín's crimes were responses to maltreatment at the hands of

Americans. Thus the political dimension of the myth—its embodiment of the anxious and ambivalent relationship between the conquering Americans and the resentful, subjugated Californios—is concretely represented in the personal suffering of Joaquín.

In addition to specifying the political theme, the *Herald* piece added other particulars that built up the image of Joaquín as a Romantic hero: he came "of good family," had received an "excellent education" and had formerly been "of quiet, modest, and honorable character." The depredations of the American writer's "lawless and ruffianly countrymen," however, had destroyed that once noble character, though the writer admires him still as "a *bravo,* a *valiente.*" The writer explicitly ties the "gay robber" Joaquín into Spanish tradition: the bandit has no doubt been influenced by legends of famous robbers and he "pictures to himself their dashing triumphs and their heroic end, meeting death without fear, and immortalized in robber annals."

Doubts about the truth of this story were immediately aired in other newspapers. An anecdote, often repeated over the years, told by this "Joaquín"—that he had written, over a "Wanted" poster in Stockton offering $1,000 for his capture, "I will give $5,000—Joaquín"—was immediately exposed as a fable by someone who pointed out that such a reward had never been posted in Stockton. That this tale was contrived is further suggested by the pat moral the writer draws: he clearly sees Joaquín as an emblematic victim of the mistreatment of immigrants and Californios occasioned by the Foreign Miners Tax, with drinking and gambling and moral disorder among the miners the unhappy consequence. Miners who succumb to the lure of drink and gaming and lose all they have "become as reckless and as insolent" as the Mexican, "and their lives henceforth [are] given to pleasure and brawls." This disorder is "an indication of the fever which rages in the social and political system of California, which some say is tearing her very vitals out."

Clearly, this version of Joaquín is an allegory for the social conditions of California, where an influx of disreputable adventurers exploit a weak and corrupt political and social order. The victims of such ruffians, like Joaquín, in turn become forces of disorder. Joaquín thus represents the moral confusion reigning in California and threatening its very existence, a disorder that demands a political solution.

On May 7 the *San Joaquin Republican* confirmed the *Herald* story and gave Joaquín a surname: "Muliati," an obvious corruption of Murieta. A few more pieces of the legend were added: he "spoke English fluently," always had a "fresh horse at hand," and was supposed to have said that he "would never kill a Spaniard."

The construction of Joaquín's persona was advanced by another report that appeared in the *New York Tribune* on June 14, 1853, and was attributed to a correspondent in San Francisco. The story notes the legislature's act establishing the Rangers and the $1,000 reward, and connects the manhunt to the widespread political corruption in the state: the act establishing the rangers "will serve as an excuse to tap the already well depleted Treasury of this unfortunate state." It then tells the tale of Joaquín, generally following the *Herald* account.

Joaquín is now of "Spanish descent" and "well-educated," details consistent with the earlier accounts' use of the bandit as representative of the Californios rather than the recent Mexican arrivals. Indeed, this Joaquín is "one of those who welcomed Americans and American rule in California—but unfortunately one who has been despoiled over and over again of his property" and "had his dearest rights invaded and trampled under foot by those scoundrel ruffians found in all our new settled regions, who alike disgrace our nation and common humanity." This more accurately portrays the experience of the Californios than that of the Mexican immigrants. As does the *Herald* version, this one sees in the bandit's story an allegory: the villains have alienated decent, American-loving Mexicans like Joaquín who, "his love turned to hate, with all a Spaniard's burning revenge ... has sworn eternal warfare against everything and person American." The writer ends with an expression of admiration for Joaquín's "prowess and manly bearing, his intelligence and sagacity."

These newspapers stories about Joaquín establish thematic personal traits, particularly his intelligence, chivalric manners and good education, all of which would contribute to his mystique. And they establish also his motive: mistreatment at the hands of Americans, including the violation of his property and personal rights and the humiliation of a flogging. This theme of vengeance situates Joaquín in the middle of the political conflict between parvenu

Americans and the old Californio ruling class, who like Joaquín were being despoiled of their rights, particularly the property rights guaranteed by the Treaty of Guadalupe Hidalgo, and who also like Joaquín were suffering humiliation at the hands of Gold Rush riffraff. The sympathy these accounts show for Joaquín and by extension the Californios suggests that some Americans were disturbed by the alienation of the respectable Californios, who should rightfully be allies in establishing civil order.

So these first accounts are moralizing allegories speaking to the extraordinary social conditions of the time, and the ambivalence some Americans felt in their relations with the Californios. It is these fictions that will later be recycled as historical fact. The catalyst for this process was a novel written by a half-Cherokee journalist who saw Murieta's story as a mirror for his own trials and tribulations.

TWO

Social and technological changes were creating a wide audience for popular romance. The invention of the steam-driven rotary press and techniques for manufacturing cheap paper, along with the spread of literacy and circulating libraries, permitted a new genre of popular literature called "penny dreadfuls" and later "dime novels." The first penny dreadfuls, such as *Lives of the Most Notorious Highwaymen, Footpads, etc.* and *The Calendar of Horrors,* both serialized in 1836, were filled with violence, savagery and torture. And they were wildly successful.

These lurid tales exploited the taste for the exotic created by Romanticism, particularly the enthusiasm for criminals and highwaymen reflected in gothic novels, in the eighteenth-century *Newgate Calendar* and in the works of poets like Byron and Schiller. In 1840, for example, *Angela the Orphan: or, The Bandit Monk of Italy* sold fourteen thousand copies a week. Real-life criminals such as Jack Sheppard, Dick Turpin and Claude Duval were all subjects of popular novels throughout the first four decades of the nineteenth century. Respectable novelists such as Charles Dickens and Edward Bulwer-Lytton also indulged the public's fascination with crime and the social or genetic conditions engendering it. A common motif of these stories was that of the basically goodhearted man driven to crime by circumstances beyond his control—a figure typifying the now widely popularized Romantic revolt against respectability and social conformity. And heroes like Robin Hood and Sir Walter Scott's Rob Roy were portrayed as taking up arms against political and ethnic oppression.

William Harrison Ainsworth was a very popular novelist in the early nineteenth century who exploited the public interest in daring criminals and their crimes. Ainsworth combined several influences: the historical novel as fashioned by Sir Walter Scott; the late-eighteenth-century gothic novel; and the "rogue novel," all spiced with generous doses of gruesome violence. Ainsworth's *Jack Sheppard* (1839) is particularly significant for Ridge's novel. The hero Jack, an apprentice, is an intelligent, engaging orphan who mutates into a criminal after enduring abuse and humiliation at the hands of his master's shrewish wife, the final insult coming when she slaps his face while Jack is trying to alert his master that some visitors are actually criminals. "May I be cursed," Jack vows, "if ever I try to be honest again." In the romance Jack is paired with a criminal of pure evil, Jonathan Wild, an actual criminal about whom Henry Fielding had written a novel in 1743. This narrative of the basically good man driven to crime by circumstances beyond his control, juxtaposed with the criminal whose evil is unmitigated, will recur in Ridge's novel, where Murieta's foil will be the brutal Three-Fingered Jack.

The conditions creating the vogue for this kind of story certainly existed in California. Literacy was widespread, and the gold country was flooded with periodicals—in 1850, there were fifty printers in San Francisco, and by the mid-fifties the city published more newspapers than did London. Weekly journals combining fiction and poetry with news were also popular. The *Golden Era* had eleven hundred subscribers in the northern mines, and it frequently ran stories about dashing highwaymen who always acted chivalrously toward women. The popular taste for tales of crime found an obvious subject in Murieta even before Ridge's novel. In May of 1854 the first number of the *Pacific Police Gazette* started a serial called "Joaquin the Mountain Robber, or the Bandits of the Sierra Nevada." Unfortunately, a disgruntled printer murdered the editor, and the series died. No copy has survived. In July of that year another crime tabloid, the *California Police Gazette,* ran a serial called "Joaquin the Mountain Robber: or, the Guerilla of California"; only two chapters have survived, so it is difficult to judge what influence it had on Ridge's novel, published the following month.

That the shadowy criminal Murieta was being viewed through the stained glass of popular Romance was obvious to many in California, including the newspaper writers who were principally responsible for concocting the Romantic persona for him in the first place. In February of 1853 the *Sacramento Union* had compared Joaquín to the Scottish Highland rebel Sir Roderick Dhu from Scott's poem *The Lady of the Lake.* Later in August the *Alta California* would snort that the "renowned robber chief Joaquín" had been "made a great hero of romance by newspaper writers and legislators." This "supposed romantic chieftain" was "purely a fabulous character." Such realism, however, could not compete against the appetite for Romance soon to be exploited by a journalist and poet whose life was even more fabulous than the fiction he created.

THREE

John Rollin Ridge came from a family of Cherokees who intermarried with whites and who believed that assimilating to American culture through education offered them the best chance to avoid the fate of other tribes who had stood in the way of westward expansion. His grandfather, Major Ridge, in 1813 had fought with the federal government under Andrew Jackson against anti-assimilationist Creeks called Red Sticks. A fervent believer in education, in 1821 he sent his son John, father of John Rollin, to school in Connecticut, where the young man fell in love with the daughter of a white nurse who tended him when he fell ill with scrofula. Two years later they married, despite fierce opposition from the town.

John Ridge returned to northern Georgia, where his father owned a 280-acre plantation near Ridge's Ferry. Now a lawyer, he was prosperous enough to build his own plantation near his father's, a 419-acre estate called Running Waters. Born there in 1827, John Rollin was educated by a woman from Massachusetts who ran a school at Running Waters. It was a time of increasing tensions with whites, who begrudged even assimilated Cherokees their prime farmland and wanted them to migrate to Indian Territory in the West. At first uniting in their resistance, the Indians and their leaders soon divided over how to respond to the increasing pressure. The party lead by John Ross wanted to resist—though by political rather than by forceful means. John Ridge on the other hand supported the move west, and signed a treaty that compensated the Cherokees with $4,500,000 and over 13 million acres of land in Arkansas, to which the Ridge party duly trekked, arriving there in the fall of 1837.

In June the following year, the federal government began the forced emigration of the remaining Cherokees that has come to be known as the Trail of Tears. About four thousand Cherokees died during the nearly yearlong march, including John Ross's wife. The survivors harbored bitter resentment toward those who had signed the treaty and emigrated earlier. In June 1839 this bitterness led to the assassination of John Ridge and his father, Major Ridge, by hotheads loosely aligned with the Ross faction. John Ridge was dragged from his bed, and in full view of his family, including John Rollin, was stabbed twenty-nine times and then ritually stamped upon by all twenty-five men in the band. As John Rollin later wrote, the death of his father "darkened my mind with an eternal shadow."

After two years at school in Massachusetts, Ridge married a white woman, studied law in Fayetteville and began writing Romantic poetry. He brooded on the terrible injustice he had suffered and fantasized constantly about "a deep-seated principle of revenge in me which will never be satisfied until it reaches its object." The simmering feud between the Ross and Ridge factions probably lay behind a quarrel over a horse that ended when John Rollin killed a Ross man who had gelded one of his stallions. The outcome was that in 1850, along with his brother Aeneas and a slave, but leaving his wife in Arkansas, he joined a wagon train for California.

Once in the gold country, Ridge quickly grew sick of the backbreaking drudgery of mining. He became a correspondent and "travelling agent" for the *New Orleans True Delta.* He began publishing in other periodicals as well, including the *Golden Era* and the *Alta California,* using his Cherokee name, "Yellowbird." Ridge also published numerous poems in which the travails of his own life found Romantic expression: his obsessive thoughts of vengeance, his exile and separation from his wife and his status as a Cain figure fleeing a killing. Ridge finally found steady employment as the deputy clerk, auditor and recorder for Yuba County, north of Sacramento.

Ridge's work as a journalist no doubt made him familiar with Joaquín's crime spree. Moreover, the fragments of information about Joaquín presented in the newspapers—above all the injustices suffered by Murieta and his thirst for revenge—resonated with Ridge's own experience and appealed to his Romantic sensibility.

He also needed the money, and he naturally assumed that the sensational story of Murieta and his grim death could be turned to advantage, given the period's taste for highwaymen and gallant assassins. Thus in August 1854 he published a ninety-page book with thin paper covers, *The Life and Adventures of Joaquín Murieta, The Celebrated California Bandit,* giving the amorphous myth of Murieta its most enduring form.

FOUR

Ridge's first paragraph locates his novel in the popular literature of his day. He links Murieta—"a man as remarkable in the annals of crime as any of the renowned robbers of the Old or New World"—to the long tradition of "rogue" literature. His claim that his novel will someday contribute to the "early history of California" appeals to the vogue for historical novels most famously exploited by Sir Walter Scott. He piques his era's curiosity about the origins of crime with the statement that Murieta "was nothing more than a natural production of the social and moral condition of the country in which he lived." And he does not fail to indulge the predilection for murderous action with an allusion to the "dark and horrible in human action."

As were Harrison Ainsworth's novels or the penny dreadfuls, Ridge's story is pure fabrication. This has not prevented many historians from treating his novel as a primary source for presumably factual history.

Ridge begins his tale with an account of Murieta's youth. His raw materials are clearly the newspaper accounts discussed above, especially the *San Francisco Herald* story of April 18, 1853. As in that account, Ridge's Joaquín came from "respectable parents" and was "educated in the schools of Mexico." He had a "very mild and peaceable disposition" and a "generous and noble nature." Disturbed by the unsettled conditions of Mexico, he decided to journey to California and "try his fortunes among the American people, of whom he had formed the most favorable opinion." So, "fired with enthusiastic admiration of the American character," the young Joaquín is hard at work by 1850, successfully mining in the Stanislaus placers.

The author's physical portrayal of Murieta likewise derives from the newspapers. It seems to combine the Nahl engraving of April 1852 and the postmortem description published in the *San Joaquin Herald* in August 1853. Ridge's Joaquín is "a little over the medium height, slenderly but gracefully built, and active as a young tiger," a phrase recalling the *Herald*'s "sprightly as a cat." Yet the "large black eyes," the "firm and well-formed mouth" and the "long, glossy, black hair" evoke Nahl's engraving. This description better fits Ridge himself than the Murieta described by the Rangers, who was blue-eyed and fair-skinned.

The literary sources for Ridge's story multiply as he spins his tale. Like the author of the *Herald* piece, Ridge condemns the "lawless and desperate men, who bore the name of Americans but failed to support the honor and dignity of that title." He likewise associates the depredations of such thugs with the crude ethnocentrism of uneducated American miners. But it is Ridge's own experience as a well-educated "half-breed" who is looked down upon by ignorant whites that comes through in his condemnation of "the prejudice of color, the antipathy of races, which are always stronger and bitterer with the ignorant and unlettered" and that afford excuses for "unmanly cruelty and oppression." As did the journalists, Ridge sees Murieta's story as a parable of California's unfair social conditions. But he sees another allegory as well: one that describes his own wrongs and sufferings at the hands of lesser men.

Next occur the three injustices that launch Joaquín on his bloody career. First a band of "lawless men" drive him from his claim, slapping his face and then, while he watches bound hand and foot, raping his "heart's treasure," the Sonoran girl Rosita. He tries farming, but again "a company of unprincipled Americans—shame that there should be such bearing the name!"—drives him away. Finally, he ends up at the small Gold Rush town of Murphy's as a monte dealer. Here a mob wrongfully lynches Joaquín's brother for stealing a horse, and "[binds Joaquín] to a tree, and publicly disgrace[s] him with the lash." At this point Joaquín, like the antihero Jack Sheppard after he is slapped, is transformed: "Then it was that he declared to a friend that he would live henceforth for revenge and that his path should be marked with blood." This last phrase resembles the *Herald* Joaquín's vow that his "track shall leave a trail of blood."

No evidence has been found that such injustices were ever actually experienced by the historical Joaquín. Most crimes, especially the relatively rare crime of rape, and most lynchings were reported in the many newspapers published around the gold country, and no reports have been found documenting the lynching of Joaquín's brother or the rape of his wife. Literature, however, does provide models. The flogging episode appears in the *Herald* story and provides a believable cause for Joaquín's rage, since vigilante justice frequently included corporal punishment. Another literary model could have been an incident described in the *Shirley Letters,* published serially in 1854–55 by the *Pioneer,* whose offices were no doubt frequented by Ridge, a contributor.

"Dame Shirley" was a New England woman named Louise Clappe who attended Amherst with Emily Dickinson. In 1849 she moved with her husband to California, ultimately living at Rich Bar on the Feather River. Her "Letters" are valuable and insightful descriptions of everyday life in the mines, written in the Romantic idiom of the day.

One of her stories, dated August of 1852, involves the aftermath of a fight between some Spaniards and an Irishman who ended up dead. A vigilance committee was elected, and it sentenced two of the Spaniards to be whipped. One of the Spaniards, "young" and "gentlemanly," begged to be killed rather than suffer "the never-to-be effaced stain of the vilest convict's punishment." Rebuffed, "he swore a most solemn oath, that he would murder every American that he should chance to meet alone." The similarities to Ridge's Murieta, who also vows revenge against Americans after he is whipped, argue for Dame Shirley as a more likely source than historical fact. Another possible source available to Ridge is the previously discussed *New York Tribune* article of June 1853, in which Joaquín is reported to have "sworn eternal warfare against everything and person American." An unrelated press report of a whipping near Diamond Springs was actually altered in a later county history to include Joaquín; in this version the bandit, "a fine-looking man ... bowed to the people with a smile, saying in English: 'Gentlemen, I am as innocent of this stealing as any of you.' "

Pointing out these literary or journalistic antecedents for Ridge's episode does not mean that the historical Murieta did not suffer some insult or indignity at the hands of Americans, as did many of his countrymen. But it remains true that there is no historical basis for attributing his crimes to anything other than greed and a penchant for violence.

Another literary influence may be the popular historical novels of Sir Walter Scott. Earlier we noted a newspaper article comparing Murieta to Scott's Sir Roderick Dhu. Scott's world of Celtic Highlanders battling the oppressive Anglo-Saxons had obvious analogies with the Californios and Mexicans, who likewise turned to banditry in order to resist an ethnically and religiously alien power. One novel by Scott particularly suggestive for Ridge's work is *Rob Roy,* in which the Scottish outlaw Rob Roy McGregor plays a minor role. Coming out in 1817, *Rob Roy* was hugely successful, selling ten thousand copies in two weeks. In the novel Roy's various illegal activities, including cattle-stealing, blackmail and smuggling, are seen as legitimate responses to the onerous excise taxes and general oppression brought by the English and their supporters. As a Scotsman says to Francis Osbaldistone, the novel's hero, such activity is "a mere spoiling o' the Egyptians," an allusion to the goods the Israelites took with them when they were liberated from Egypt. And Rob's wife is raped by his enemies, just as Murieta's is in Ridge's novel. Scott's romance could have provided Ridge with a model easily translated to Gold Rush California.

Exploiting the rumors of a Mexican rebellion against American rule that had appeared in the press, Ridge likewise describes Murieta as a nascent revolutionary. At one point he announces to his men that he is at "the head of an organization ... of two thousand men." He intends to "arm and equip fifteen hundred or two thousand men and make a clean sweep of the southern counties" and to "kill the Americans by 'wholesale,' burn their *ranchos,* and run off their property." Only then will his own wrongs and those of "our poor, bleeding country" be avenged. Ridge later connects this conspiracy to "many wealthy and influential Mexicans residing" in California, from whom Murieta had "received assurances of their earnest co-operation in the movement which he contemplated." As we saw earlier, Harry Love cited an identical canard in order to extend his commission with the Rangers. Murieta as revolutionary is a warning of the larger consequences of the treatment Ridge and his people had endured.

Another device in Ridge's novel with literary antecedents is the character of Three-Fingered Jack, considered by many to be based on Bernardino Garcia, the man who during the Mexican War allegedly tortured two American soldiers by feeding them their own flesh. Just as Ainsworth's *Jack Sheppard* uses the real-life outlaw Jonathan Wilde as the exemplar of pure, unmotivated evil that contrasts with the more conflicted character of Sheppard, so Three-Fingered Jack is presented by Ridge as a vicious, sadistic killer—"cruel and sanguinary" and "utterly destitute of one merciful trait of humanity." While Joaquín is tormented by the humiliations he has suffered and his fall into banditry, Jack's "delight was in murder for its own diabolical sake."

The monstrous Jack served to explain away the innocent victims of the historical bandits, particularly the many Chinese miners whose throats they slit, who in fact as a group suffered more persecution and exploitation than did Mexicans. After Joaquín rescues a "Celestial" from Jack, the killer muses, "I love to smell the blood of a Chinaman. Besides, it's such easy work to kill them. It's kind of a luxury to cut their throats." The newspapers had anticipated Ridge's contrast of Joaquín and Jack; the *San Joaquin Republican* in August 1853 detailed Jack's life and career and concluded, "Joaquin was a saint in comparison to the other demon."

The bulk of Ridge's novel, with its numerous gun-battles and murders, hairsbreadth escapes and chivalrously treated damsels in distress, all described in overripe prose, bespeaks its origins. His contemporaries immediately recognized the novel as an imaginative Romance having little to do with the actual Murieta. In August

1853 the *San Francisco Daily California Chronicle,* comparing Ridge's Murieta to Jack Sheppard, noted that "the fancy [imagination] of the author is undoubtedly equal to the style of his writing." The reviewer pointed out that "if the lives of all the Joaquins that ever cut a purse could be written, they would not contain the horrid catalogue in this book." The reviewer went on to doubt that Murieta was killed by Harry Love, as did many people when Love made his claim—a charge the novelist resented, as it impugned his veracity. He immediately published a response in the *Daily Placer Times and Transcript* detailing the extensive newspaper research and interviewing he claimed went into the novel. Ridge did take many incidents and actual people from the newspaper reports, but the trouble is that those reports are frequently unreliable and confused.

In fact, Ridge's novel springs from the popular literature of his day, and from his own fantasies of vengeance against those who murdered his father. Ridge's Murieta tracks down and kills the thugs who abused him and his wife, a closure the author never enjoyed. Murieta's sufferings and isolation clearly embody Ridge's vision of himself as a Romantically tragic figure. The novel itself does not substantiate the author's claim that it is "strictly true," and it certainly should not be used as a source of information about the historical Joaquín.

At any rate, Ridge's hopes for a bestseller apparently came to naught. In a letter from October 1854, he claimed that the publishers sold seven thousand copies and "putting the money in their pockets, fled bursted up *tee totally* smashed, and left me, with a hundred others, to whistle for our money!" These sales figures are dubious, since only one copy of the novel has survived. No more credible is his assertion that the publishing house went bankrupt, since in 1855 it was still in business a few blocks from its old location. Ridge also said he had prepared a second edition, but there is no evidence that such a work ever materialized. He went on to establish several newspapers, edit others, press the federal government for land for the Indians and write poetry until his death in 1867 from "softening of the brain." He was forty years old.

John Rollin Ridge never made money from the Joaquín legend. But he did bequeath a model that has reappeared down through the years: the fictionalization of a shadowy history that can be used to communicate the author's own psychological obsessions and political agendas and that may find a hospitable environment in the social and political ferment of the day.

FIVE

Subsequent nineteenth-century literary incarnations of Joaquín continued in the main to indulge the popular taste. As American rule was consolidated in California and social institutions began to strengthen, the anxieties over relations with Californios and foreign immigrants, apparent in newspaper accounts and Ridge's novel, hardened even further into the clichés of melodrama. Murieta became a figure of pure Romance that appealed predominantly to Anglo readers searching for a history of the new state.

In 1858 Charles E. B. Howe published in San Francisco *Joaquin Murieta de Castillo,* a play that managed to outdo Ridge's reduction of Murieta into a stock character. No records have survived that show the play was ever produced or even reprinted, but it could have been intended for amateur theatrical groups. The fact that it was written at all indicates that at least Howe believed the subject to be one of interest to English-speaking Californians.

Howe adds some intriguing embellishments to Ridge's novel, from which he lifts whole sentences unchanged. He makes the young Murieta, now living in an orphanage in Mexico, heir to a Spanish dukedom and its great wealth. The boosting of Murieta as educated and chivalrous that appeared even in early newspaper reports has here reached its acme, testifying to the hold that Romantic preconceptions had on the nineteenth-century imagination. The aristocrat as elegant outlaw was an especially popular theme. The literary journal *The Golden Era,* which published Ridge as well as Mark Twain and Bret Harte, ran a story in December of 1852 about an Austrian baron who held up coaches and, like Murieta, was always chivalrous toward the ladies who fell into his power. The "good address" of Governor Bigler's reward proclamation had evolved into noble birth.

The same outrages that turn Ridge's Murieta into a killer reappear in Howe's play, only this time his wife, renamed Belloro or "Golden Bell," and pregnant to boot, dies of shame after she is raped by the miners, who are all characterized as illiterate drunken bigots.

Joaquín's onetime admiration for Americans turns to hatred as he begins killing his tormentors and plotting a revolution to retake California for Mexico. As in earlier incarnations, Howe's Murieta is a sympathetic character driven to crime by the social elements that were attracted to the mines and scorned by the respectable Americans who doubtless would have made up Howe's audience.

A decidedly anti-Catholic subplot is the only innovation Howe brings to the Murieta legend. His villain is the renegade priest Gonzalles [*sic*], known as the "Fighting Priest" for his depredations as a guerilla during the Mexican War. Gonzalles, lusting for Murieta's fortune and estates back in Spain, engineers the hero's death by betraying him to a Ranger named Byrnes. This anti-Catholic sentiment perhaps reflected the brief influence of the nativist Know-Nothing party, which whipped up support by exploiting fears of Catholic and Jesuit domination and paranoia over growing Irish political influence and corruption. By 1854 the Know-Nothings controlled San Francisco, Stockton, Marysville and Sacramento, and in 1855 they took all the statewide offices, including the governorship. By 1857, however, the Know-Nothings were out of power. In a state with so many foreigners and Catholics, especially in southern California, the Know-Nothing program could not last. Its defeat testifies to the distaste crude chauvinism aroused in the more respectable Californians, a distaste that partly accounts as well for the popularity of Joaquín, the victim of foul-talking, bigoted riffraff addled by drink.

The next incarnation of the Murieta legend, while unexceptional in itself, is important because translations of it were the basis for the many later editions popular in Spain and Latin America. In 1859 the *California Police Gazette* serialized the Murieta story in ten issues, then published the whole as a pamphlet titled *Joaquin Murieta: The Brigand Chief of California.* This was illustrated by Charles Nahl, whose 1853 engraving in the *Sacramento Union* had depicted a large-eyed, swarthy, hawk-nosed Joaquín. His engravings for the *Police Gazette* likewise fixed the image of Joaquín as a dark mestizo, despite the published eyewitness descriptions of the bandit as blue-eyed and fair-skinned.

The *Police Gazette* version is an unabashed plagiarism of Ridge's novel, as Ridge frequently and fruitlessly complained. There are a few changes. Murieta's early history now includes a stint as General Santa Anna's groom in Mexico City, another example of the folklore motif that causes famous people to cross paths. Murieta's wife is now called Carmela, and after her murder (a departure from Ridge, who has "Rosita" survive her disgrace), he finds solace in the arms of a mistress named Clarina. This change in names establishes the *Police Gazette* as the source of subsequent plagiarized versions and foreign translations, most of which have Carmela and/or Clarina rather than Rosita as Murieta's consort.

These knockoffs of Ridge's work have little intrinsic value, testifying merely to the century's boundless enthusiasm for the genre. Typical is the version published in 1865 by Henry Llewellyn Williams in the DeWitt Fifteen-Cent Library: *Joaquin (The Claude Duval of California); or, The Marauder of the Mines.* Williams took most of his material from the *Police Gazette* version (Murieta's consorts are Carmela and Clarina), reworking it to conform more specifically to the conventions of crime novels like *Jack Sheppard.* Thus Williams compares Joaquín to a whole roster of famous European criminals and highwaymen, but gives the Californian preeminence over all of them. And Williams continues the pretence of historicity: his account, subtitled a "Romance founded on truth," is based, he tells us, on "contemporary witnesses" and "official documents." The novel combines scenes of gruesome violence and saccharine sentimentalism, all delivered in purple prose and alliterative bombast such as "Red-handed Ravager" and "Pirate of the Placers." Williams gives the game away at the end when he confesses, "Perhaps we have colored the facts a little vividly."

More interesting is the use to which the Joaquín myth was put by the poet Cincinnatus Miller, who became known as Joaquin Miller, the "Byron of the Rockies," but who is largely forgotten today. Miller was born in Indiana in 1837, and at the age of fifteen accompanied his parents in a wagon train to Oregon. In 1854 he left home for California, where he mined near Mount Shasta. He lived with Indians for a while, was involved in some fights with them and was wounded in the face with an arrow. He also witnessed the Pitt River Massacre of 1857, in which starving Indians were killed in retaliation for an attack on whites. Arrested for stealing a mule, he escaped from jail and for a while was an express rider. During the Civil War he edited a pro-Confederacy newspaper, started a short-lived literary review and ultimately was elected judge. But his ambition was to be a Byronic literary figure, an ambition his mediocre talent made improbable. Failing to impress literary San Francisco with his first book of poems, despite the recommendation of Bret Harte, Miller sailed to London where in 1871 he stumbled across fame with a self-published collection called *Songs of the Sierras.* Included in the book was a long poem called "Joaquin Murietta."

Miller's success in London no doubt reflected the English taste for American Noble Savages, who had for centuries made convenient sticks with which to beat a jaded, corrupt European civilization. As the *Westminster Review* wrote, "We ourselves prefer the roughness of the backwoods of America to all the drawing-room conventionalities of Europe. We prefer Mr. Joaquin Miller's native reed-pipe to any guitar." Joaquin certainly dressed the part, with the long hair, sombrero, tall boots and sash of the California *vaquero.* And he wasn't averse to embroidering his biography to enhance his Western persona. The nickname "Joaquin" and the poem about the dashing Mexican bandit no doubt added to his allure, evoking the glamour of blasted youth, shocking violence, exotic locales and doomed love—the staples of lowbrow Romantic literature.

Miller's poem, however, much like Ridge's novel, is less about the bandit Murieta than about the Romantic sensibility that found in him a dramatized manifestation of its own longings. Miller's Joaquin is predictably pensive and melancholic, with his "long silk locks of blackest hair," his "raven curls" and a brow seeming "to hold a tale of woe"; it is a "brow of blended pride and pain, / And yearnings for what should have been," and there is a "glory in his eye / That seems to dare and to defy / pursuit." The description of Joaquin's unnamed consort is equally ripe, with purple patches like "soul-deep eyes of darkest night." The bulk of the poem is divided between the speaker's description of himself thinking about the bandit in wild, sublime California landscapes, and the bandit's farewell kiss of his woman, which is drawn out to tedious lengths in order to mine every last nugget of emotion.

In the 1892 edition of *Songs of the Sierras,* Miller added a note that purported to redeem this bit of bombast with history. He speaks of the "gross wrong to the conquered Californian," forgetting that

Murieta was in fact not a Californio but a Mexican immigrant. Miller concludes, "The splendid daring and unhappy death of this remarkable youth appeal strongly to me; and, bandit as he was, I am bound to say I have a great respect for his memory." Yet the poem is about nothing other than Miller himself; and Joaquín is the myth of his own life, the outlaw and quasi savage rebelling against a corrupt, mediocre society.

As in Ridge's novel, the assertion of the self and its exquisite sensibility is hidden behind a scrim of historical fact. The references to the injustices suffered by Joaquín and other Mexicans validate the pursuit of self-expression by yoking it to the larger, nobler cause of social justice. Both Ridge and Miller illustrate a perennial trick of the Romantic sensibility: the smuggling of self-absorbed individualism within the baggage of a rebellion against injustice that is ostensibly waged on behalf of victimized others.

While Miller's poetry about his namesake was diverting London's drawing room set, John Rollin Ridge was preparing a new edition of his novel, which eventually came out in 1871, four years after he died. He called it a third edition, perhaps counting the plagiarized *Police Gazette* version as the second. His new preface, in addition to complaining justifiably about the theft of his work, keeps up the pretense of historical truth, claiming that he has enlarged his earlier work "according to the scope of additional facts, the knowledge of which has been acquired" since the first edition. This conceit allows Ridge to set his new edition apart from the plagiarizing "spurious work" with all its "fictitious additions."

Ridge's additions are themselves fictive elaborations of earlier scenes and insertions of new adventures typical of the genre. The success of the *Police Gazette* and the DeWitt Fifteen-Cent Library versions apparently suggested to him that he should, as the anonymous authors of those had done, make the violence more graphic and the sentiment more fervent. Thus he fills in the background to Rosita and Joaquín's relationship, making her the daughter of a packer who works for Joaquín's father. She becomes Joaquín's mistress and then runs off with him to California. And the scene in which Joaquín is slapped and Rosita raped is fleshed out with graphic details and heightened drama: after the slap, Rosita grabs Joaquín's bowie knife and attacks the miners. Other additions chronicle not newly unearthed historical facts but blood-soaked adventure fantasies. If violence and romance were what readers wanted, Ridge would give it to them.

Apparently that was just what readers did want. Ten years after Ridge's third edition the Beadle's Dime Library published three Murieta novellas, all by Joseph E. Badger: *Joaquin the Saddle King* and *Joaquin the Terrible: The True History of the Three Bitter Blows That Changed an Honest Man to a Merciless Demon,* both published in 1881; and in 1882 *The Pirate of the Placers; or, Joaquín's Death Hunt.* These are predictable melodramas, with cardboard villains prone to colorful curses such as "Ten thousand devils fly away with the sluggish rascal!" Comically hackneyed as they are, these productions testify to the continuing fascination of the Anglo reading public with a Gold Rush past ever receding into the fog of nostalgia and fictive memory. And the phrase "True History" in the title suggests that myth and history were now inextricably mingled, with history fading into the conventions of light fiction.

By century's end, this mythicizing of history gained added force from the changes in California that followed the end of the Gold Rush and the coming of the railroads. The 1870s were particularly disruptive; as historian Kevin Starr describes that decade, it was "an unmitigated disaster of drought, crop failure, urban rioting, squatter wars, harassment and murder of the Chinese, cynical manipulation of politics by the railroad, depression, price fixing, bank failure, and stock swindles." No wonder that in the century's last two decades the way of life on the great *ranchos* and the adventure of the Gold Rush were frequently extolled. To Romantic Anglos, the Californios and Mexicans of that period, like the eighteenth-century Highland Scots, "combined the romance of a primitive people with the charm of an endangered species." This aura of regret for a lost, better world pervades a long poem (seventy pages of rhyming couplets) from 1882, in which Joaquín figures as a paragon of olden times: Marcus A. Stewart's *Rosita: A California Tale.*

Looking back on the Gold Rush days, Stewart celebrates California as "Earth's last and loveliest paradise," and the Santa Clara Valley as a "vale of plenty, peace and love." In that region the poet imagines Joaquín's wife Marie and friend Rosita, consort of Joaquín's trusted lieutenant Ramon, standing by the brigands' signal fire on Mt. Loma, brooding over their endangered lovers and soothing one another with Spenserian stanzas sung to the guitar. Murieta is fulsomely described as: "The first and fiercest in the fray," and he is a "captain worthy to command / The wildest desperado band / That ever trod our golden land." In couplet after couplet turgid with adjectives and predictable rhymes, Stewart creates a Joaquín and a California as unreal and contrived as any medieval romance. Once more we see, as in Miller's poem, Joaquín's role as representative of that lost pastoral world more chivalric and adventurous than the grubby California created by the railroads and industrial wheat farming, a California where now "year by year the hand of man, / Convulsing Nature's happy plan, / In dull ambition would revise / What first was formed a paradise." To Stewart, Joaquín is an extension of that lost exotic landscape, "the wildest spirit of the scene."

The bandit's story, as Stewart has him narrate it to his gang, pretty much follows the plot laid down by Ridge and subsequent versions, except Stewart ends with Joaquín and Marie in Mexico, mourning their dead comrades Ramon and Rosita. By now any point about the historical injustice suffered by Mexicans and Californios has been lost in the flood of sublime posturing. Ravaged womanhood, youthful innocence wrongly injured, regret over the fall from noble character, the thirst for revenge—all are occasions merely for sounding a plangent note.

The impulse to embroider the past crops up as well in the supposedly more factual reminiscences of men associated, either directly or indirectly, with the California Rangers and the manhunt for Joaquín. Ranger Bill Byrnes, who recognized the bandit and was said to have gambled with him in the Gold Country, was interviewed at the age of forty-eight in May of 1872 by the *Sacramento Union;* understandably he magnifies his role in the pursuit and capture of the criminals. He adds some new features, such as his claim that Murieta was betrayed by a few drunken members of his gang, some Indians, and a woman who had a grudge against him. Byrnes takes credit for cutting off the heads and the hand, but tells a sorry tale of how he left them in the care of an old Mexican War buddy, who was supposed to change the whiskey while Byrnes went for alcohol.

But the war buddy drank the whiskey, and Jack's head, deteriorating rapidly because of the gunshot wound, had to be buried.

In an interview with the *Fresno Weekly Expositor* in November of 1879, Ranger William J. Henderson, who shot Murieta, provided a version of events that dressed up the facts with touches of fiction. Henderson claimed that Joaquín had lived in Sonora with one Colonel Acklin. He was driven from his claim by two Irishmen, one of whom struck him in the face with a whiskey bottle. Henderson, as did the early fictions that were probably his source, attributes Joaquín's criminal career to this insult. However, he "laughs at the idea of the old story that Joaquin was induced to seek a course of crime because of mistreatment of his wife," since Joaquín never had a wife. Describing the final battle, Henderson claims that he recognized Joaquín by the scar on his cheek, thus corroborating his story of a wound inflicted by a whiskey bottle. It seems unlikely, however, that in the excitement of the pursuit Henderson would have noticed such a scar; nor can we credit his claim to have administered the coup de grâce with a shot through the heart.

Horace Bell was a veteran of the Civil War and of the Nicaraguan adventures of William Walker, most famous of the "filibusterers," that is, those Americans who attempted to seize land by force in Latin America. Bell was a Los Angeles Ranger and a famed fabulist whose highly embroidered memoirs contributed yet more particulars to the growing Murieta legend. Bell was not a member of the original California Rangers, not having joined the Los Angeles Rangers until 1856. He later became a lawyer, superintendent for Indian affairs in California and Nevada and publisher of a weekly called the *Porcupine,* in which many of his tall tales were first published. In 1881 he published his *Reminiscences of a Ranger,* the first clothbound book to be wholly printed and published in Los Angeles. As Arthur M. Ellis, the editor of the 1933 version, delicately puts it, Bell suffered from a "tendency toward exaggeration." His reminiscences about Murieta were indeed creative.

Bell's most significant contribution—one that would become central to the incarnation of the myth prevalent in the 1960s—is to perpetuate the idea that Murieta was actually a political rebel fighting an oppressive American occupation. The old canard of the bandit's extensive and well-organized network is recycled by Bell, who claims that Murieta possessed a "degree of executive ability and genius that well fitted him for a more honorable position than that of chief of a band of robbers." Bell suggests that anywhere else "the operations of Joaquin Murietta would have been dignified as the title of revolution, and the leader that of rebel chief." He repeats the earlier newspaper account that Joaquín had been "educated in the school of Revolution in his own country," and speculates that Joaquín "felt himself to be more the champion of his countrymen than an outlaw and an enemy of the human race."

Bell's other figments are literally fantastic. He tells of a Los Angeles character named simply Bill, who had known Louis Napoleon, the Duke of Wellington, Don Carlos and "King Gumbo Jumbo of Timbuctoo." Bill, according to Bell, was a secret agent for the United States government during the Civil War whose mission was to make sure that pro-Confederacy Los Angeles stayed in the Union. With such a roster of famous acquaintances, Bill is of course also linked to Murieta, who was his "chum" in 1852 when the bandit resided in Los Angeles, before the murder of General Bean. Alas, Joaquín suspected that Bill was enjoying "over-intimate relations" with the bandit's sister Vincenta. Joaquín was taking a chance in confronting Bill, since "Bill knew Murietta's movements, and could've betrayed him, had not *Vincenta* and honor protected him."

The reminiscences of aging lawmen can be forgiven for their colorful touches. We can also expect to find in the memoirs of famous men looking back on their youth the impulse to enlarge their place in history by linking their own lives to those of other notables. John C. Frémont, in his memoirs published in 1887, told the story of a "handsome lad, eleven years old" named Pablo Hernandez, whose parents were killed by Indians east of Los Angeles in 1844. Frémont took the boy east with him and lodged him with Frémont's father-in-law, Senator Thomas Hart Benton. Despite the Benton family's efforts, however, "the root of [Pablo's] character seemed strongly bad," and the boy disappeared. Frémont said he later heard that Pablo had gone to California and that he and the robber chief Joaquín Murieta were one and the same.

Other California pioneers as they aged somehow managed to draw on associations with the famous bandit. Major Edwin A.

Sherman, Mexican War veteran, miner, lawyer and surveyor, reported in his memoirs penned near his death in 1914 that he met Murieta and his gang while returning from a surveying expedition near the Merced River. "I recognized the leader as Joaquin Murieta, a dreaded bandit," Sherman wrote. He invited the gang to breakfast, and true to the mythic characterization of Murieta as the gentleman, the gang "courteously partook of our hospitality" and then rode off, leaving Sherman and his party unmolested. Four miles downstream they discovered the gang's victims, three corpses with gunshot wounds and slit throats.

Sherman's anecdote is similar to many that developed in California among Anglos, in which Murieta is cast in the role of Robin Hood. One story told of a woman whose husband was out riding with the posse that was pursuing him. The bandit comes to her home on the very day the bank was threatening to foreclose on it. He breakfasts with the woman, hears her story, then reveals himself—after giving her $2,200 to pay the bank. Other stories tell of people spared by him because they had helped him in the past, of ladies having their property returned, and of horses "borrowed" from ranches with sacks of gold dust left in their place.

Every Californian of note seemingly had some sort of connection with the gentleman. Edward Fitzgerald Beale was a naval officer who survived the battle of San Pascual, brought to Washington the first sack of California gold, was Lincoln's surveyor general for California and Nevada, and later served Ulysses S. Grant's administration as minister to the Austro-Hungarian Empire. He acquired the vast Tejon Ranch north of Los Angeles, where for a while he managed a model reservation whose aim was to teach Indians how to farm and become self-sufficient. Talking with the journalist Charles Nordhoff in 1872, Beale claimed that after it was severed the head of Murieta was brought to his camp at Tejon—an invented memory recognizably false by anyone familiar with the location of the shootout and the head's journey to Fort Miller, far to the north of Tejon. And by his own testimony elsewhere, Beale was in Utah when Murieta was shot.

Autobiographies and memoirs are notoriously unreliable, but the major histories of the state that appeared in the late nineteenth century were no more careful at sorting out truth from fiction. In

1888, for instance, Hubert Howe Bancroft, dean of California historians, published his *California Pastoral,* the very title of which attests to the sentimentality that frequently mars its pages. In his discussion of Murieta, Bancroft gives the stamp of scholarly veracity to outright wish-fulfilling fantasies. He validates the interpretation of Murieta as a resistance fighter battling that "encroaching and heretical neighbor, the insolent gringo," against whom brigandage was a "chivalric ideal." Having established an exculpatory context for Murieta's crimes, Bancroft goes on to paint an equally clichéd portrait of the bandit: "Joaquin was of gentle blood, and as handsome and gay, and chivalrous as any youthful knight-errant." He uncritically repeats the formulaic mythologizing of John Rollin Ridge and other dime novelists, including the slap on the face, the rape of his wife, the lynching of his brother, the degrading whipping and the vow of vengeance.

This mawkish performance works up to a flowery description of the desperado's "slender figure, and graceful limbs, and large black eye, and long black hair": he is a "perfect Apollo, richly dressed, blooming in the pride of health and manly beauty." Bancroft's historiographical malfeasance is glaringly evident in this description, since a brief look at contemporary newspaper accounts immediately postdating the bandit's death would have contradicted the assertion that he had black hair and eyes.

Ten years later, Theodore H. Hittell published his multivolume *History of California.* Hittell, while he recognizes that most of the information about Murieta derives from "unreliable reports," nevertheless goes on to rehearse Ridge's basic narrative, which he repeatedly cites in his notes as his source! What Hittell rejects is not the mass of pseudo-facts but the naïve idealizing; thus he dismisses all the reports of Murieta's chivalrous magnanimity, even though they derive from the same sources as the spurious details he *does* accept. To Hittell, Murieta is a "vicious and abandoned character, low, brutal and cruel, intrinsically and at heart a thief and cut-throat," although an "anti-foreigner persecution" has made him "worse than he would otherwise have been." Like Bancroft, Hittell makes factual mistakes that could easily have been avoided by looking up contemporary newspaper accounts, such as his assertion that Murieta killed General Bean in Los Angeles, a blunder also found in Ridge. Despite his halfhearted reservations, Hittell sums up by stating that he has reported the "main facts." In such fashion are dreams foisted upon history.

SIX

While the historians were busy transmuting myth into history, the folklore concerning Murieta was growing apace. The several versions of Murieta's life and death bequeathed a figure that fit neatly into the outlaw archetype, which became increasingly popular toward the end of the century as the Wild West retreated ever more rapidly into the past and became the subject of mass-produced entertainment. His type came to represent a revolt in the name of individualism against the new economic and technological forces altering the American landscape. In a world of increasing economic and political complexity, conformity and corruption, the outlaw was, according to historian Richard Meyer, "a people's champion who espouses a type of higher law by defying the established 'system' of his times." Meyer goes on to identify twelve elements of the outlaw paradigm, all of which fit Murieta perfectly, as they do Jesse James and Billy the Kid.

One of Meyer's elements is the persistent skepticism about an outlaw's death. The confusion over the identity of the bottled head encouraged this tendency in the case of Murieta. Some of the doubt expressed in contemporary newspapers can be chalked up to political feuds, since Governor Bigler's enemies in the press dismissed the Rangers and their activities as so much pork barrel payoff of doubtful utility to the citizenry. But rumors that Joaquín had not been killed at Cantua Creek repeatedly cropped up in subsequent years. Harry Love reportedly admitted in a Santa Clara saloon a few years after the gunfight that he had not even been at Cantua Creek when the bandit was killed, and when asked whether the head was Murieta's, simply shrugged. Bill Byrnes allegedly said that "one pickled head was as good as another if they [*sic*] was a scar on the face and no one knew the difference." Another story has Byrnes refusing the reward because he knew the head wasn't Murieta's, and many other persons over the years made the same assertion.

The doubts were encouraged by a steady stream of Murieta sightings. He was seen in San Luis Obispo, San Jose, Placerville,

Mexico, Chile and Peru. In 1855 it was put about that a letter existed claiming that Murieta and eleven men were returning to California in order to wreak vengeance. The next year a Santa Cruz paper announced his return. In some versions he dies peacefully of old age in Sonora, in others he is killed during one of Mexico's many revolutions. In 1879 a priest in Tucson, Arizona reported that in 1857 he had officiated at the marriage of Joaquín's brother; the latter showed the priest a letter from Joaquín, instructing him to keep repeating the bogus story of his death. In the 1970s the writer Stan Steiner, on a visit to the Mexican state of Sonora, was shown the purported grave of Murieta in the ruins of a Jesuit church.

One of the most charming tales came from the son of B. F. Marshall, a sheriff in Calaveras County who claimed to possess a photograph of Murieta given to him by the bandit after Marshall had rescued him from some ruffian miners. (The fact that this photograph was made with a process, either ambrotype or tintype, not in use until after Murieta's death has not prevented it from being reprinted even to this day.) According to Frank Latta, Marshall's grandson F. B. Marshall claimed his grandfather had kept a diary covering the years 1850–53. The diary was lost, but F. B. said his father had copied and rewritten portions of it recording Murieta's rescue. Such tortuous evidentiary journeys cast strong doubts on the veracity of the information, particularly since the entries are highly flattering to B. F. and repeat legends consistent with Ridge's novel.

Marshall's son told the story as he heard it from his brother-in-law, Miguel Araz. In Tuolumne County Araz knew an old man with long flowing hair and a white beard; he spoke good English and kept a herd of pigs. This preposterous character spent his time wandering around with his pigs and digging small excavations, until suddenly he vanished. One day a certain Italian, who had kept a store in the Gold Rush town of Hornitos during Murieta's time, told Araz that in a tavern in Brazil he had been approached by an old man with white hair and beard, who questioned him about Murieta; the Italian said he remembered him as a generous patron who always overpaid for his food and drink. This personage, of course, identified himself as Murieta, and Araz realized that the two ancients were one and the same, and that he had been searching for his buried gold, which in the end he had found.

The search for Murieta's horde of stolen gold was yet another leitmotif vivifying the legend. Calculations from newspaper accounts, assuming Murieta was responsible for all the crimes, give a total of around $21,000 in gold. This figure increased exponentially over the years as treasure hunters scoured the state.

In 1883 the *Fresno Expositor* reported that a map existed detailing where $100,000 in gold was buried: Three-Fingered Jack had given the map to an old priest. In some versions the ghost of the priest delivers the map to a "Mrs. Joaquin Murieta." In 1890 the *San Francisco Examiner* said that an Australian, David Wall, whose father had been killed by Murieta and who had been taken care of by "Joaquin's sweetheart," had dug up the treasure in Santa Barbara County and returned home with it. In 1893 a hustler, appropriately named Felix Sharps and armed with maps and diagrams, convinced a consortium of San Francisco merchants that he knew the location of the treasure, which he said was near the Yuba River. Convincing them that he should head an expedition to recover the gold, he fleeced them of $2,800. In Yuba County, Murieta himself gave an old miner a map leading to a "fortune in diamonds and gold"; and in the town of Chico, $42,000 was said to be buried under the porch of a certain ranch house.

Over the years numerous "secret caves" in California were tracked down with the aid of "ancient maps," frequently yielding not treasure but the skeletons of murder victims. In 1906 three boys tumbled into a cave west of Angels Camp and found a rusty knife, large-rowelled spurs of the sort favored by *vaqueros,* and a one-shot derringer. The *San Francisco Call* proclaimed: "Murietta's Refuge Discovered in Calaveras County." A man from Santa Rosa named Kirkpatrick nursed the last member of Murieta's band, who drew him a map to the buried millions. In 1928 a biography of ninety-eight-year-old Ranger William Howard, source of much Murieta mythology, claimed that Rosita had buried the gold near Howard's ranch; and several years later, according to Howard, three mysterious Mexicans appeared and searched in vain. One Major Baldwin from England eventually discovered the gold.

As late as 1968 a gold hunter's guide called *Lost Treasures and How to Find Them!* started off with Murieta and his hidden millions. In the 1970s, the magazine of the National Treasure Hunter's League reported that two hundred pounds of gold—$15,000,000 worth—had been buried by one of Murieta's henchmen near an oak tree with an "X" carved on it. Naturally, many of these yarns of buried treasure featured ghosts that watched over the trove and either frightened the seeker away or assisted him; one story in *Sunset Magazine* told of some Indians who had discovered Murieta's gold near Tejon Pass but had been frightened away by his shade.

Easily the most fascinating bit of Murieta-related folklore is found in the story of Mariana Andrada, also known as Mariana la Loca ("Crazy Mariana"), who called herself his widow and lived near Three Rocks in order, some believed, to search for his gold. According to a Mrs. Teodora Arredondo, who herself claimed to be the widow of a packer who had transported supplies for Murieta, the attractive and lively Mariana Andrada came to California in late 1852 or early 1853. She worked in dancehalls, some say as a prostitute. She began to boast that she was the widow of Joaquín.

Much of her subsequent life is unknown; but in 1875 she was interviewed in a shepherd's hut near present-day Avenal in Kings County by *San Francisco Chronicle* reporter Boyd Henderson (who was with a posse pursuing the notorious Tiburcio Vásquez, a robber active in the early 1870s who became something of a celebrity before he was hanged). Once she was well oiled with whiskey, Mariana claimed that Joaquín was nineteen when William Henderson killed him, and that he was a *güero*—light-complexioned with blue eyes and fair hair. She also said that Joaquín in a fit of rage had given her the large scar across her face when she ran off with one Charlie Baker; that Mariana and Joaquín had a son, living in Mexico; and that the bandit was buried nearby, though Mariana didn't offer to show the grave to the reporter.

Mariana's story is without doubt pure fantasy. According to Arredondo, Mariana got her scar in a tavern brawl—though one can reasonably question Arredondo's own reliability, since she was over one hundred years old when Frank Latta interviewed her in 1933.

Mariana reentered the historical record several years after the *Chronicle* interview when she started preaching in the area of Three Rocks, near the spot where the Rangers had killed Murieta. By 1883 Mariana was prophesying the end of the world and claiming to be in contact with Father Magin, the "Holy Man of Santa Clara" who had died in 1830 and whose life was being investigated by a Catholic commission in order to certify his sanctity. As word of Mariana's cult spread, throngs of Mexicans, along with some French, Portuguese and Basques, some selling all their possessions, flocked to Cantua Creek just below the Joaquín Rocks to hear the supernatural voice of Father Magin speaking from one them (Mariana or a male accomplice doubtless providing the voice).

The voice of the holy man passed on the information that he was over eight hundred years old and had been buried in the middle of the three Joaquín Rocks. A *Fresno Expositor* reporter who visited the encampment found five hundred people living in tents and brush houses or simply beneath the sky. The believers said that soon the Joaquín Rocks would be miraculously transformed into a cathedral. Meanwhile many sick people were healed with leaves plucked from a nearby "Tree of Life." Mariana warned her flock that the world would end exactly on May 16, 1886: the San Joaquin River and Buena Vista Lake (southwest of present day Bakersfield and now dry) would flood and kill everyone in the Valley, and China would sink into the sea. The reporter groused, "It was all a humbug."

Mariana's ecstatic movement came to an end a couple of years later when in July 1885 she was charged with murdering an infant whose death she had prophesied. She was tried in Fresno and acquitted. Abandoning her millennial cult, Mariana took to drink, her antics earning her the nickname "Crazy." In 1902 she was killed by a train near the east Valley town of Hanford.

SEVEN

While authors and raconteurs of various stripes were keeping the legend alive in California, versions of the story were appearing in Europe and South America. Joaquín and his exploits were apparently well known in his home state of Sonora, where Murrieta was and still is a common surname. In 1872 an American engineer named Albert Owen passed through the town of Hermosillo in Sonora while searching for Topolobampo Bay on the Gulf of California. Owen was surveying for a railroad and he dreamt of making the bay, thought to be suitable for a port, its terminus. According to his diary, while in Hermosillo he attended a play called *Debt of Honor* by an otherwise unknown playwright named Don Gabutti. In his diary Owen mentions another play by Gabutti called *Joaquin Murrieta,* and repeats a few details about Murieta, some of which are incorrect: he places his death in the fall of 1854, and confuses Three-Fingered Jack with Joaquín Valenzuela. He also mentions that two of Murieta's brothers were living at Buenavista on the Yaqui River.

Owen's brief description of the play suggests that Gabutti followed the standard story; indeed, it is possible that he simply adapted or translated Howe's play of 1858. Owen tells us that he made Joaquín a "hero of the first water" and that the play was quite bloody, the only character left alive at the end being the prompter. He notes that Americans and other foreigners were afraid to attend the play, and after a production "gringos" were frequently "insulted" in the streets of Hermosillo. The testimony of Owens suggests that at least in northern Mexico, Murieta by the 1870s was viewed as a heroic resistance fighter and a victim of Yankee aggression. Yet the facts of his life and exploits reported by Owen—his wife ravaged by a "party of roughs" and his gold stolen by "American cut-throats"—derive not from local history but from the usual American sources. The presence of a popular literary version of Murieta's life this early in Sonora calls into question the authenticity of later family legends told to historians like Frank Latta by Joaquín's Sonoran descendants.

Joaquín was known elsewhere in Latin America. A French translation of the *Police Gazette* version done by one Robert Heynne in 1862, *Un bandit californien (Joaquín Murieta),* was translated into Spanish by the Chilean Carlos Morla Vicuña in 1867 and published in Santiago. Murieta in this incarnation became *"el bandido chileno."* Apparently the book was a great success, for it went through fourteen editions, as well as being incorporated into a huge work by Carlos Nombela y Tabares, "*La fiebre de riquezas; siete años en California*" (*The Fever of Riches: Seven Years in California,* 1871–72). A serialized version, never completed because the Spanish-language weekly *La Gaceta* ceased publication, appeared in California in 1881. At some point Heynne's book was reprinted in Barcelona, Spain, and in Mexico, and in 1906 a longer version was published in Barcelona under the authorship of Profesor Acigar. All these editions derive from the *Police Gazette* version.

The transformation of Murieta into a Chilean created a version of the myth that has endured, as we shall see, to the present. Many Chileans came to California during the Gold Rush, since the ships rounding Cape Horn on the way to the gold fields visited the port of Valparaiso in Chile. Like other Catholic and Hispanic immigrants, Chileans who came to California were subjected to harassment and abuse by ignorant American miners who indiscriminately lumped all Hispanics together as "greasers."

In July of 1849, San Francisco's Chile Town, a tent city in a ravine near Telegraph Hill, was attacked and sacked by the Hounds, the gang of Irish thugs who practically ran the city for a couple of years. One Chilean died. The so-called "Chilean War," in December of 1849, near the Calaveras River at Chile Gulch, pitted Chileans against American miners who had ordered them to leave on the grounds that the Chileans used forced labor. During the altercation several men were killed; as a result a few Chileans were lynched, some were whipped and others had their ears cropped. Decades later memories of these atrocities would make Murieta an attractive hero for Chileans, particularly toward the end of the century when "Yankee imperialism" seemed to be expanding throughout the hemisphere.

Another Spanish offspring of the *Police Gazette* was published in 1904 in Mexico by Ireneo Paz, the grandfather of Octavio Paz, the Mexican novelist and essayist. Paz changed Murieta's nationality back to Mexican. This version sold well, a fifth edition being published in Spanish Los Angeles in 1919, testifying to the interest in Murieta on the part of Hispanic Angelenos. Paz follows the *Police Gazette* reworking of Ridge, with the same claim to authenticity that characterizes the legend from the start.

Paz does change the hero's final words, having him say as he expires, "You have taken me by surprise, I say, but it's not important! I die satisfied.... I have already avenged myself enough!" This statement highlights both his nobility and his motive of revenge for dishonor, a theme no doubt of interest to Mexicans on both sides of the border. In one edition Paz ends by mentioning three sisters of Murieta said to be still alive in Los Angeles, even publishing their photographs. In 1925 Frances P. Belle translated Paz's novel into

English, thus bringing the *Police Gazette* version of the Murieta legend back full circle to its origins.

Joaquín's symbolic value has always been more important than historical truth. For Hispanic Californians, both the dwindling Californios and more recent immigrants, Murieta represented the injustice inflicted upon them in the past and the present, and his bloody acts of vengeance functioned as collective wish-fulfilling fantasies.

EIGHT

By the beginning of the twentieth century, the basic elements of the Joaquín myth were fixed and from then on were repeated over and over again; for in Murieta's story was concentrated for Californians the Romantic vision of their past and the way they negotiated its contradictions and complexities.

The creation of the "new" California—a product of railroads, suburban development, real estate speculation, Midwestern immigration, oil, agribusiness and the nascent film industry—was attended by the creation (and marketing) of the myth of the old Hispanic California, what longtime *Nation* editor Carey McWilliams has called a "fantasy heritage." Helen Hunt Jackson's popular novel *Ramona* (1884), a tale of star-crossed Indian lovers and idealized *rancho* life, reflected the perennial taste for Noble Savage exoticism and nostalgia, no matter how false to reality. The title alone of Gertrude Atherton's *The Splendid Idle Forties* (1908) testifies to the appetite for manufactured mawkishness about the past. John McGroarty's *Mission Play* (1912), which enshrined life in the Spanish missions, played to 2.5 million people in seventeen years and, like *Ramona,* became an annual civic pageant and opportunity for chamber of commerce boosterism. By the twenties, many cities were staging annual "Spanish Fiestas" in which "Californios" rode mounts resplendent in silver and Anglo girls were elected *"señorita."* Santa Barbara, during its "Spanish Days" fiesta, put on a play about Murieta, and in San Francisco another pageant told the story of the "California love bandit."

Through the figure of Murieta, Californians could put their Hispanic heritage on a pedestal and distance themselves from the darker realities of their past. The base lowlifes who brutalized Joaquín and his wife and turned an essentially noble character into a killer embodied what was sordid and mean in California history: squatterism, or the racist lynchings, or the Foreign Miners Tax—unpleasant historical realities that detracted from an ideal that was being incorporated into Anglo-Californian identity.

Two examples, one from popular and the other from academic history, illustrate this process. George H. Tinkham's *California Men and Events* (1915) repeats substantially the Ridge and *Police Gazette* versions of the legend, though Tinkham does add that Murieta came to California with the circus, a detail perhaps picked up from an *Overland Monthly* article published in 1909. In telling Joaquín's story Tinkham emphasizes the actions of xenophobic whites: "Ignorant, degraded whites began a series of insults, abuses and maltreatment of the foreigners, and the innocent and the guilty alike suffered." Thus the "bloody career of Joaquin Murietta and his gang was due is some measure to the brutality of a party of white men." In the same manner Richard Mitchell's M.A. thesis at UCLA in 1926, *Joaquin Murieta: A Study of Social Conditions in Early California,* despite its scholarly apparatus likewise interprets Joaquín's crimes—the story of which is lifted wholesale from Ridge, cited as a source—as the consequence of prejudice against foreigners and the Miners Tax. Again the ignorant, greedy rabble is condemned.

In both popular and academic work, then, history becomes a simple melodrama of injustices perpetrated by the wrong sort of people who flourished during the social chaos of the Gold Rush, and upon whom all the sins of that era can now be heaped by modern Californians eager to recover and market their glamorous Mexican past. If the Mexicans and Californios were somewhat improvident and hedonistic, they are nonetheless exemplars of a passionate approach to life, manifesting a love for romance and adventure increasingly rare in the California of suburbs and railroads.

This recycling of the Murieta myth was attended by further additions that were incorporated and that helped maintain its vitality. In 1919 Frederick R. Bechdolt reprised the Ridge version for the *Saturday Evening Post.* A popular anecdote retold by Bechdolt concerns the chain mail that newspapers said Joaquín wore. When he purchased the armor from a Frenchman, the story goes, he first made the salesman put it on and then fired a pistol at him. Having proved the chain mail's efficacy in stopping the slug, the bandit cheerfully paid up.

In 1921 a piece by May S. Corcoran in the *Grizzly Bear* started off by rejecting the Robin Hood persona—"our bandit left no record of merry moods"—but ended with an overripe description of Joaquín fleeing just days before his death. The bandit stops for a drink near Mariposa, bending his face "to the purple anemones and cooling maiden-hair of the little spring." He then sees his own reward poster, and catching the sound of a "violin and harp playing a Spanish waltz," he rides to the dance for a last waltz. Those who recognized the bandit "drew courteously aside until, the dance ended, with a bow he left them." Even for skeptics the pull of Romance was too great to resist.

One of the gaudiest retellings of the Joaquín story was concocted by Evelyn Wells, who published it in a supplement to the *San Francisco Call* from December 1923 to February 1924. Wells starts with the by now obligatory claims to historical accuracy, asserting that the series was the fruit of her travels through "every corner of California known to '49" and that the story, though "it may not all be true . . . comes direct from the lips of his [Joaquín's] friends." As the historian Joseph Henry Jackson noted, those "friends" would have been ten years old when they consorted with the bandit, and eighty when Wells interviewed them in 1923.

After this historiographical throat-clearing, Wells's story of the man she calls the "Napoleon of banditry" follows the *Police Gazette* version in which Rosita dies from the outrage inflicted upon her. But she adds numerous new elaborations, evidently chosen for their degree of violence or mawkishness. Joaquín rides with strings of human ears around his saddle horn, and Three-Fingered Jack, an "idiot murderer" who "bit the hearts of his victims, tore off their heads," was fond of tying his Chinese victims together by their pigtails. Wells links Murieta to every California Gold Rush figure and every bit of Gold Rush lore she can find, weaving a history for a state that, having sprung into existence almost overnight, seemed to lack one.

For example, we find that while in San Francisco, Joaquín has a run-in with the famous Hounds. And that John Marshall, Sutter's employee who made the original discovery of gold, sees Joaquín in the Valley after he is supposed to be dead. As we read Wells with her fanciful connections, we realize that she is summing up (and marketing) the legendary past of California through the agency of Joaquín: he has become a figure whose mystique for Anglo readers defines the California allure.

A few years after Wells's performance, in 1927, Joseph Gollomb, a prolific writer of true-crime "histories," published *Master Highwaymen,* in which Joaquín appears beside such stars as Dick Turpin and Jack Sheppard as "America's Super-Bandit." Despite the mandatory reference to "much hunting among dust-covered records," Gollomb's Murieta—a "picture of romance," he admits—is the standard fiction. This author does come up with a few new twists. Joaquín, always a well-educated desperado, now between raids reads Racine and Cervantes in his "mountain fastness." Gollomb ups the ante of the miners' brutishness, having them rape Carmela while she is unconscious, and he has Carmela stab herself to erase her shame. The finale is depicted as a duel between a knife-wielding Joaquín and Captain Love, resplendent in the uniform of the nonexistent "California State Militia." Love drills the hero through his broken heart as the bandit leaps towards him.

Surviving Rangers likewise provided new grist for the mythic mill as they touched up their place in California's imagined history. In 1928 Jill Cossley-Batt published *The Last of the California Rangers,* a biography of Ranger William Howard "from materials furnished by himself, chiefly through spoken narrative." Howard had died four years earlier at the age of ninety-eight, exercising to the last his fertile powers of invention for the credulous Cossley-Batt.

Howard's account, in fact, is a compendium of all the various literary inventions that had accumulated around the figure of Murieta in the previous seventy-five years. Howard's memories fashion Murieta even more explicitly into the type of the heavily sentimentalized hero, a "dark-skinned boy of seventeen with dreamy-looking eyes" who elopes in "true Lochinvar style" with Rosita, a "dear Castilian maiden, with pure ivory skin, deep black eyes, and hair smoothed down with oil of almonds, possessing all the dignity, beauty, and lure characteristic of the daughters of Spain." Rosita, also known as "Queen" for her beauty, was a crack shot too, engaging in shooting contests with Captain Howard for bottles of champagne, a pastime that aroused the jealous suspicions of Joaquín. The reference to Scott's Lochinvar suggests the Romantic paradigm through which Howard is reinventing Murieta—indeed, he explicitly links Murieta to Scott's Richard the Lionheart and the Waverly novels.

Howard's other details locate him firmly in the by then rampant outlaw genre. California Ranger Bill Byrnes, who identifies Joaquín before the gunfight, is called by Howard "a noted card player" and an old friend and "ex-partner in a monte game" with Joaquín, thus adding the element of betrayal to Byrnes's identification of Murieta at Cantua Creek. Betrayal by a onetime friend is a consistent motif of the outlaw myth. And in calling Murieta the "California Robin Hood," Howard evokes the theme of economic redistribution; the comparison persists down to the present day despite the absence of any evidence showing that Joaquín and his gang ever shared their plunder with the poor. Expanding on the legend of Murieta as political rebel, Howard calls him "El Patrio, the man who was going to bring California back under the Mexican Eagle"—another perennial fictional role for Murieta. One can understand why Howard, like Love half a century earlier, inflates Murieta's significance: it inflates as well his own role in thwarting this potential revolutionary.

Howard commits errors of fact that he (or his biographer) could easily have avoided by consulting old newspapers. For example, he repeats the story of the phantom "Dead or Alive" reward poster in Stockton upon which Murieta allegedly scrawled an even larger offer. And he follows Ridge in making Murieta responsible for the death of General Bean, whom Howard has Murieta roping off his horse and stabbing to death as Bean was returning from reviewing "two companies" of militia called up to pursue the bandit—a more dignified activity by far than the real Bean's drunken stroll home after pawing an Indian woman.

Howard's most radical deviation from the historical record occurs in his description of the fatal gunfight. According to Howard, the Rangers kill twelve of the "swarthy desperadoes," who are surprised during their "siesta," the afternoon nap these bandits were presumably enjoying at dawn right after sleeping all night. When Murieta is cornered, Ranger White wounds him in the hand. Joaquín holds up the hand "in token of submission" and says, *"Mira mi mano, amigo,"* that is, "Look at my hand, friend." Ranger White is "too chivalrous to take advantage of a wounded man" and announces, "I arrest you." At this point, unfortunately, some bloodthirsty Rangers rode up and "shot the bandit to pieces." For some reason Howard has left Ranger Henderson completely out of the shooting and ennobled the behavior of Ranger White.

Our old friend Horace Bell was not finished supplying fanciful details of his own. In 1930 he published *On the Old West Coast: Being Further Reminiscences of a Ranger,* a work as inventive as his first book nearly fifty years earlier. In his new reminiscences Bell tells of a portrait of the bandit, frequently reproduced even today, purportedly painted by a priest at Mission Carmel a few months before Joaquín's death. The latter had hidden out there after being routed by Captain Love and his posse near San Jose. According to Bell, the priest sent the painting to an American woman in Los Angeles, to be passed on to Joaquín's sister. Thirty years later Bell acquired the painting along with the priest's accompanying letter, after the woman had died and Bell was settling her estate. When Bell had the painting restored, the artist recognized the subject as Joaquín because he had seen the severed head on display in New York. But there is no record of the head ever being displayed in New York, and Bell does not reproduce the corroborating letter.

In folklore, formal history, popular history, magazine articles, fiction and poetry, the figure of Joaquín first created by newspapers and Ridge's novel—factual errors, imaginative inventions and all—was reproduced over and over again and taken as historical fact. In 1932 a novel and later a film would bring the legend to its largest audience yet.

NINE

Walter Noble Burns's *The Robin Hood of El Dorado* was not the first appearance of Joaquín in early-twentieth-century fiction. In addition to Belle's translation of Ireneo Paz's novel, several other authors were attracted to the Murieta mystique. A member of the Mexican consulate in San Francisco, Adolfo Carrillo, published in 1922 a collection of stories called *Cuentos Californianos,* which contained a tale called "Joaquín Murrieta." Carrillo, following the folkloric need to connect famous persons, invents an episode in which Murieta attends the wedding of Mariano Vallejo's niece. (This same requirement would later make Murieta the lover of the famous chanteuse Lola Montez.) He also has Joaquín's sister Dorotea, not his wife or mistress, abused by the miners, who are led by an Australian convict named Pat King. Consistent with the Judas theme often found in this kind of folklore, Carrillo has the bandit betrayed by a kiss from his quisling girlfriend, Lina Solana. Otherwise, Carrillo follows the basic Ridge/*Police Gazette* formula.

Superior court judge Ernest Klette's *The Crimson Trail of Joaquin Murieta* (1928) and Charles H. Snow's *The Sheriff of Chispa Loma* (1931) are also unexceptional reworkings of the Ridge/*Police Gazette* versions. In both these novels Murieta (called Juan Moreno in Snow's novel) is viewed sympathetically, as the victim of demonized *gringo* miners given to saying things like "Nothin' suits me better, if there's a chance of stretchin' up a greaser." And in both novels, the Spanish culture of preconquest California is idealized as an exotic, sensuous world that to twentieth-century Anglos remained deeply attractive, albeit in need of a dose of redemptive Protestant work ethic.

Two other novels that worked Murieta into their plots are likewise occasions for daydreaming. *A Plaything of the Gods* (1912) by Charles Park turns Murieta into a native Californio with "royal blood from both sides of his house," that is, both Spanish and Aztec. The first part of the novel is set in the mission school where Joaquín is being educated by a priest, who intends the youth to be a cultural leader against the "swindling gringos." But outrages against Joaquín and his Castilian bride, Carmela Felix (the name collapsing the Ridge and *Police Gazette* names for the bandit's consorts), turn the youth into a vengeful force on behalf of Mexicans and Californios "who had been robbed of their lands, driven from their homes and beggared, and . . . whose sisters, daughters or sweethearts had been ravished by the cursed gringo." Their wrongs avenged, the bandits turn to "helping the helpless"—Robin Hood and his Merry Men. Park's innovation in the story is to have an aging yet still charming Murieta drown himself in a lake to free his young third wife so she can unite with her lover.

Whereas Park indulges the myth of the missions, Lanier and Virginia Stivers Bartlett's *Adiós* (1929) focuses on the quasi-medieval fantasy of the *rancho.* Their Murieta, now called Don Francisco Delfino, is the Californio heir to a huge estate. The novel begins when he has just returned from several years in Mexico, where he fought the Americans at the battle for Mexico City. The authors leave no doubt about their estimation of the *rancho* world, "Those halcyon days of the most complete freedom that perhaps any community of human beings ever enjoyed." The easygoing, pleasure-loving *rancheros* are contrasted with the money-grubbing, gold-obsessed *gringos* who cause the noble Francisco to metamorphose into the legendary bandit, Puma, accompanied by his faithful retainer and "ugly old Sancho Panza," Three-Fingered Jack.

Walter Noble Burns's *The Robin Hood of El Dorado* (1932) contains just about every bit of Murieta lore circulating at that time. Burns was a Kentuckian who sailed on a whaler, fought in the Spanish-American War, worked as an editor at the *Chicago Tribune* and wrote several novels about the Wild West and its outlaws. Though by far the best-written of Murieta novels to that time, Burns's version is no more based on fact than its predecessors, despite its author's journalistic training. Yet Burns casts his novel as accurate history, and even suggests its contrast with the "sentimental veil of poetry" that enwraps the bandit, who is now "a picturesque figure of fantasy, high-souled, as chivalrous as he is brave," the "Robin Hood of El Dorado."

For his part, Burns carefully creates an impression of historical accuracy based on empirical evidence. He makes reference to interviews with old-timers who possess Murieta relics such as a dagger or a sash soaked with his blood; preserved documents in the California State Library; unreliable historians like Bancroft; yarn-spinners like Horace Bell and B. F. Marshall, he of the spurious photograph (which Burns calls "perfectly authentic"); and tall tales said to be "of indisputable authenticity."

Burns provides details about Murieta, his thoughts and his conversations that were obviously concocted in his own imagination, as in his claim that Murieta's "military machine" had "headquarters, general staff, field forces, and an army of spies and secret agents." As his own title suggests, and despite the patina of historical reliability, when all is said and done Burns has recycled an imaginative construction of the Murieta legend essentially identical to its earlier literary incarnations, with the same combination of saccharine romance and shocking violence.

As did earlier sentimentalists, Burns employs the legend as a device for delving into California's colorful past, larding his story with numerous digressions about the Gold Rush and its lore, including anecdotes about Mark Twain and Bret Harte, gold-mining towns, vigilance committees, bandits, lynchings, hanging trees, famous eccentrics and characters like the preacher who, while officiating at a funeral and noticing a nugget found by a miner in the open grave, staked a claim on the spot.

Burns's take on history, like earlier versions, carries a moral: he sternly judges the Americans who "burst upon the land in ruthless hordes, as voracious as vultures, to rob, swindle, bulldoze and impoverish" the Californios. The popular wisdom about the Gold Rush is fixed: contemporary Anglo Californians should prefer as their cultural ancestors the passionate *rancheros* and bandits to the repressed and gold-grubbing Yankees. Over seventy years after the Murieta myth first emerged, Burns presents the reader with the same formula delivered with the same pretensions to historical accuracy.

Some contemporary reviews of Burns's novel reflect a profound confusion over myth and history. The *New York Times* reviewer, for example, while recognizing the generic antecedents of the novel and its "breathless and lurid style," nonetheless respects as factual much of the nonsense, including the ridiculous tally of three hundred men that Murieta supposedly killed. More on the mark is the review in *Books,* which accurately places the novel in the tradition of criminal romance: "Mr. Burns has done it all in the wildest style, beating Ainsworth, Lyton [*sic*], writers of Beadles Half-Dime Library, and indeed, every one who has tried his hand at the Literature of Rascality."

Such plain common sense, however, was helpless against the charms of a fanciful California past, particularly when it became a staple of a new, dynamic form of entertainment even more powerful than the dime novel.

TEN

The Mexican people provided the young California movie industry with a host of character types and themes to exploit, many of them frankly racist: by the 1920s nearly a dozen movies had been produced with the epithet "greaser" in the title, including *Tony the Greaser, Ah Sing and the Greaser,* and D. W. Griffith's *The Greaser's Gauntlet.* The type of the Bad Mexican was usually a murderous, cowardly and/or treacherous bandit ultimately dispatched by an upright Anglo-Saxon or Nordic lawman. At the same time the idealized Mexican of the preconquest Southwest was also a favorite character: he was the Gay Caballero, a courtly, suave Robin Hood and Latin Lover. The Hispanic Avenger was also a recurring type that reflected Anglo preconceptions about hot-blooded, touchy Latins who are forever answering affronts to honor, usually involving a woman, with sword or pistol. This coexistence of positive and negative images is consistent with the ambivalence we have been tracing in the Anglo versions of Murieta, an ambivalence that faces Janus-like to the past and to the future.

Two characters embodying the rose-tinted view of Spanish California, both immensely popular in films throughout the pre-World War II period, are the Cisco Kid and Zorro.

The Cisco Kid was born in a short story by William Porter, an ex-convict who became a master of the entertaining short story under his famous pen name of O. Henry. In "The Caballero Way," from a collection of stories published in 1904, Cisco is actually an Anglo gunman loosely modeled on Billy the Kid. Set in the badlands near the Rio Grande in Texas, it tells how Cisco's Mexican girlfriend falls for the tall blond Ranger tracking him; Cisco tricks the Ranger into shooting the treacherous girl, thus wreaking vengeance on both, but not sullying his honor by slaying a woman.

Despite the fact that Cisco shoots Mexicans to death "just to see them kick," he conveniently fitted so many images about Mexicans that Hollywood transformed him into one. And whereas O. Henry's Cisco is something of a murderous psychopath, in film and radio he is transmuted into the generic Gay Caballero embodying all the glamour of early California. Starting in 1914 with *The Caballero Way,* Hollywood made dozens of movies and serials about the Cisco Kid. The radio show's writer provided him with a Mexican sidekick named Pancho whose inept buffoonery humorously confirmed preconceptions about lazy English-mangling Mexicans. When the Cisco Kid made it to television, Pancho was played by actor Leo Carillo, who appeared regularly at events like the New Year's Day Rose Parade, leading a procession of mounted *charros* or Mexican cowboys.

Zorro also was born in a short story, "The Curse of Capistrano" by pulp writer Johnston McCulley, serialized in 1919 in *All-Story Weekly.* One year later *The Mask of Zorro* was filmed, starring Douglas Fairbanks Sr. as Don Diego Vega, a Castilian Californio Robin Hood who on behalf of the downtrodden battles the minions of the wicked Governor Alvarado amid an old-California landscape of missions and *ranchos* that was familiar to movie audiences. (Helen Hunt Jackson's *Ramona* had been reprinted scores of times and had been made into four movies.) Fairbanks was coming off his successful role as Robin Hood, and his Zorro was merely the same character with a different ethnic face and in a new setting. Zorro was even more popular than the Cisco Kid—between 1929 and 1947, twenty-three movies were made about the dashing Don Diego, and McCulley kept turning out Zorro novels until his death in 1958.

All of the Hispanic character types that made Zorro popular were also present in the first film treatment of Murieta's life, *The Avenger* (1931). In that movie Murieta is a courtly bandit who serenades beautiful women. His brother having been hanged and his mine stolen, Murieta becomes the "Black Shadow" and exacts his revenge, ultimately bringing to justice the three miners who stole his claim and winning the girl.

Given the proven market for such movies, Burns's novel about Murieta was an good choice for adaptation. Putting Warner Baxter in the title role, despite his being too old for the part and afraid of horses to boot, was inspired as well, as Baxter had already twice starred as the Cisco Kid, in the film *In Old Arizona* (1929) and in *The Cisco Kid* (1931). In *The Robin Hood of El Dorado* (1936), Murieta and his gang do a lot of singing and dancing, since that was how Mexicans presumably expressed their great love of life and pleasure. And Three-Fingered Jack had already long been established as the murderous Bad Mexican in the Murieta tradition, so this ethnic stereotype could be indulged as well. The movie runs the Murieta figure through the romance wringer, adding as a character an attractive Anglo woman who rides with Murieta because she also has been robbed by the *gringos* of her father's land, upon which Joaquín once worked as a peon. After the showdown, the hero dies only after he has dragged himself to Rosita's grave.

Without a doubt the film version brought the Murieta story to a greater audience than it had previously enjoyed. As part of the film's promotion the *San Francisco Chronicle* serialized the novel in 1936, printing the last installment to coincide with the movie's premier. In Latin America too the movie rekindled interest in Murieta. In Santiago, Chile, a special supplement to the periodical *Excélsior* was published in the summer of 1936, including the Chilean version done earlier by Carlos Morla, a prologue about the bandit and a six-act play by Antonio Acevedo Hernández, at that time one of Chile's leading playwrights. The anonymous author of the prologue to the play makes it clear that the public's acceptance of Murieta, reinvigorated by the movie, was due to his status as an "anti-imperialist bandit comparable to Pancho Villa and all those who raise their rifles to defend against the greed of the north." And the play itself evokes the Latin American liberator Bolívar in a call to unite against the Yankee aggressors.

Since *The Robin Hood of El Dorado,* Hollywood has perhaps neglected the story of Joaquín, which is somewhat surprising given the growing importance of the Latino population for American culture. In the sixties the bandit did show up in episodes of a few television Westerns, including *Branded, Bonanza* and *The Big Valley.* There is also a film version of the legend released in 1965 called *Murieta,* starring Jeffrey Hunter as the bandit. The actor's blue eyes and blond hair at least make Joaquín's appearance truer to life, but the plot rehashes the various fictional devices that accrued to the legend over the years, adding the spectacular gore routinized in the spaghetti Westerns. Thus, after the hero kills the miners who murdered his wife, he is let go by the sympathetic sheriff, played by George Kennedy. When Murieta turns to banditry, however, he is tracked down by a posse led by Kennedy and dies in a nasty shootout. The device of the onetime friend who must reluctantly pursue and kill his buddy, a staple of the outlaw myth, has appeared in several Murieta novels.

Joaquín did, however, make a brief appearance in the 1998 version of *The Mask of Zorro,* starring Antonio Banderas. In this retelling of the Zorro story, the hero is actually a Californio named Alejandro Murieta, the younger brother of Joaquín. When they were boys the two orphans helped Zorro's mentor and the original Zorro, Don Diego de la Vega, escape from the evil governor Don Montero. The two boys grow up to be charming, fun-loving bandits who rob from the soldiers and give money to the poor. Ambushed by Captain Love, an American soldier whose presence in Mexican Alta California is never explained, Alejandro escapes but Joaquín and Three-Fingered Jack are surrounded. Jack is wounded and captured but Joaquín kills himself, so an enraged Love beheads him and keeps the head in a jar.

The movie perfectly recaptures old Hollywood's vision of Spanish California as a land of opulent and aristocratic dons, pert and beautiful *señoritas* and elegant, acrobatic swordsmen. The screenplay's treatment of Joaquín as a Robin Hood Californio, rather than a Gold Rush Sonoran immigrant, is squarely within the Murieta tradition. Even casting Three-Fingered Jack as Irish reflects a variation of the legend found in Richard Coke Woods's 1949 history of Calaveras County. According to Woods, Jack was an Irishman named Jack Brady who deserted from the New York Regiment and kept a collection of Chinese ears. The old Mexican character types that emerged at the birth of the movies and that quickly absorbed the Murieta legend—the Latin Lover, the Gay Caballero and the Avenger—are all recycled in *Zorro.*

More revealing is what the movie does with the character of Harry Love. That old scout and Indian fighter—in photographs he is a bear-like, gruff hulk with dark, long, greasy hair and a battered face—is transformed into a psychopathic fop, an effete, suave incarnation of pure evil with long golden locks, who keeps Joaquín's bottled head on his desk and occasionally sips from the alcohol preserving it. Whether intentionally or not, the movie taps into ambivalent attitudes toward fair-haired people in Mexican culture. As even a casual perusal of Spanish television will show, blonds evoke the ruling class and the privileged elite, and thus are frequently glamorous objects of desire and envy. Yet they also evoke the conquistadors, many of whom had fair or red hair and were the overlords and oppressors. When I was a boy, one of the favorite events for my Mexican friends was Big Time Wrestling, which featured a soft-spoken, gentlemanly Mexican wrestler named Pepper Gomez and a scraggly blond named Ray Stevens. The latter brilliantly played the part of a racist, cowardly *gringo* who fought dirty, yet when bested cravenly begged for mercy, only to ambush the chivalrous Gomez once his back was turned. I can remember the shock and dismay when an older boy said he had seen Gomez and Stevens dining together in Chinatown after the bout.

The villainous Love of the movie may in fact more closely resemble the historical Joaquín—ironically revealing the film's simplistic cultural and racial stereotyping, which is consistent with many modern interpretations of the bandit. Greedy Evil is Anglo-Saxon, militaristic, inhibited and blond. Romantic Good is Hispanic, individualistic, passionate and dark. At the film's climax, Zorro sends Love, epitome of the repressed Anglo tyrant, to a fittingly gruesome death and wins the girl. But we know the victory will be short-lived, for soon legions of rapacious *gringos* will destroy forever this many-textured, poetic world of moonlit plazas and gallant *caballeros.*

ELEVEN

Though Murieta's fame crested with the film version of *The Robin Hood of El Dorado,* he continued to provide novelists with material and to crop up in what were ostensibly factual histories. Dane Coolidge's *Gringo Gold* (1939) added little to his legend other than to rework the role of Bill Byrnes, or "Beel" as Joaquín calls him. True to the tradition, Coolidge claims that his new information is faithful to the facts, citing Byrnes's daughter as his source. According to her, Byrnes was a Texas Ranger during the war with Mexico. He was taken prisoner in Sonora, where he attended a mission school with both Murieta and Rosita. Later in the mining country he and Joaquín resumed their friendship. Coolidge is obviously elaborating on the motif of the outlaw betrayed by his friend, though Byrnes does not directly participate in the shooting of Joaquín. He refuses the "blood money," his share of the reward, and tells Love that Joaquín "was a damsite better man than most of the rangers that killed him."

Ten years later, Samuel Anthony Peeples's *The Dream Ends in Fury* also focuses on friends who become enemies through circumstances beyond their control. This author's innovation is to make Harry Love the friend and protector of Joaquín, who has to be knocked out before the miners rape Rosita and rob Joaquín. And Peeples is much more graphic in describing Rosita's rape and the numerous acts of violence. In fact, sex seems to be on Peeples's mind in his retelling of the story, reflecting no doubt the greater license beginning to be enjoyed by writers in the late forties. Thus the bulk of the novel concerns the steamy and somewhat sadistic relationship between Joaquín and his mistress, the hot-blooded La Molinera, who had appeared in Henshall's 1906 *Overland Monthly* article. After Joaquín kills La Molinera's lover, the foppish Pancho Daniell, she betrays him to Harry Love. Neither La Molinera nor Love knows, however, that Joaquín has a double, and it is actually the latter's head that is put on display. Joaquín survives to punish his treacherous mistress.

Both novelists endorse a standard interpretation of Murieta's banditry as the justified response to the treatment meted out by brutish, racist miners who continue to be depicted as bestial semi-literates given to speaking in dialect, a sure sign of lower-class status in American novels. Some historians viewed Joaquín the same way. Edwin Corle, in *The Royal Highway* (1949), a book about the El Camino Real, repeats the basic Ridge/*Police Gazette* version as fact, as well as later elaborations that were clearly untrue, such as the "Stockton reward poster" incident and the portrait, made by a priest, that was allegedly discovered by Bell. Corle is explicit about the relationship of Mexican banditry to the land grant disputes: "The highwaymen were rank amateurs; the government at Washington had found a way to rob you legally and professionally." Corle's confusion between Californios and later Mexican immigrants is a standard feature of the Murieta legend in the twentieth century.

Joaquín's more recent fictional incarnations, such as Naida West's *River of Red Gold,* Don Gwaltney's *The Bandit Joaquin* and Gary McCarthy's "Double D" Western *Gringo Amigo,* follow well-worn patterns set down by earlier novels. But by far the best fictional treatment of Murieta is Chilean novelist Isabel Allende's *Daughter of Fortune,* which follows the adventures of an illegitimate English girl, Eliza Sommers, who is raised in Valparaiso. She falls in love with an employee of her guardian's export company, Joaquín Andieta. Like

Eliza, Andieta is illegitimate, but unlike her he is poor. Yet he is intelligent and passionate and an incipient revolutionary: he has the "qualities of a natural leader" and an "electrifying personality"; he is a man "of action ... with enough clearmindedness and courage to transform ideas from books into revolutionary impulses." He "lived the torment of a political romanticism" and "was prepared to give his life for the pointless glory of a burst of heroism."

But Joaquín is also a figure from Romance, "haughty ... somber and tormented," with his "funereal pallor" and his "flashing eyes" and aura of the "tragic, damned poet." Since his poverty precludes him from both possessing Eliza legitimately and realizing his political ideals, he embezzles money from his employer and sails for California, where he will make his fortune in the gold fields. Eliza then stows away on a ship bound for California to search for her lover, accompanied by a Chinese doctor named Tao Chi'en. In California the two have numerous adventures among the *fandangos* and brothels and mining camps, where they eventually learn of a mysterious bandit named Joaquín.

Readers familiar with the Joaquín legend and its place in Chilean literature will have early on figured out that Andieta will become Murieta. His motives for turning to banditry are the same as they are in Ridge, only without the raped and/or murdered wife, and emphasis is placed on Joaquín's revolutionary fervor and passionate desire to champion the oppressed. Allende invents some variations on the legend: in her story Three-Fingered Jack is the same "swinish brute" responsible for the gang's more egregious brutalities, but now he gets his nickname after his frostbitten fingers are amputated by Eliza.

More interesting is what Allende does with John Rollin Ridge. He is transformed into Jacob Freemont, an old friend of Andieta's in Chile who becomes a journalist in California. There he invents the character of Murieta as a "Robin Hood of California," a "young man of virile mien, with the features of a noble Spaniard and the courage of a bullfighter," whose humiliations at the hands of racist miners, most of which Freemont invents, turn him into a savage killer. Freemont's goal was to write "in a heroic tone to satisfy the common man's tastes. California needed its myths and legends." Soon he was flooded with testimonials "confirming what he had written; dozens of individuals swore they had seen Murieta and described him exactly as the character Freemont had invented."

Joaquín's end follows the legend fairly closely, with the bandit ambushed at Cantua Creek and his head preserved in gin and displayed around the state. And so Eliza finally meets up with her lover, gazing at his head in a candlelit room draped with black, the pianist in a corner "thumping out funereal chords."

In *Daughter of Fortune,* Allende has perfectly captured the various attractions of the Murieta legend: the combining of revolution and romance in the assertion and creation of the self, and the way myth colonizes history until it *becomes* history. Joaquín ultimately symbolizes the role of romance and youthful idealism in self-actualization and the search for identity; and as Eliza searches the gold country for her onetime lover she is actually attempting to recapture a lost self of glamorous sexual intensity. After she and Tao Chi'en, who has become her lover, have witnessed Joaquín's head, she is able to say, "I am free." No longer wedded to an inauthentic vision of herself, she can now go forward into the real world of adult relationships and responsibilities.

TWELVE

Novelists weren't the only people fascinated by the Murieta legend. In the thirties and forties the romance and adventure of the Gold Rush attracted amateur historians eager to document a lost glamorous history for the rapidly changing state. Unconcerned with establishing the genuineness or otherwise of the information they gleaned, these tireless investigators added numerous fascinating twists to the legend of Joaquín, yet at the same time further confused folklore with fact. Representative of this process is California native J. C. Cunningham's *The Truth About Murieta,* published in 1938. Cunningham's fascination with Joaquín is understandable, as he was born and raised in that hotbed of Murieta lore of eastern Merced Country, where the landscape is filled with features like the Murrieta Buttes and the Murrieta Slough, and local old-timers no doubt were ready to spin tales about him.

Cunningham's book indeed reads like fiction rather than history; seemingly every person Cunningham meets has had some adventure with the bandit or knows some bit of Murieta lore. His main source is an employee of his father's named Big Spur. According to Big Spur, who claimed to have had many conversations with Joaquín, the outlaw was actually one Charles Ross, son of a Virginian who with his brother came to California in 1827 to work as a civil engineer, and who married a Mexican woman. After his father's death, Ross's mother remarried someone named Murieta and Charles took that name. The rest of Cunningham's story roughly follows the Ridge/*Police Gazette* pattern (Murieta's wife is named Carmela, a sure sign of *Police Gazette* influence), but with some new twists. His Joaquín falls in love with a Chilean widow named Mercedes and sends her love letters by carrier pigeons. And in accordance with the folkloric outlaw motif of surviving his supposed death, the bandit escapes the fight at Cantua Creek and dies of old age in Chile.

Cunningham adds other particulars that obey the folklore imperative, such as those linking the bandit to local figures such as William Howard, who was a California Ranger. Murieta becomes Howard's employee before he enters his life of crime, and Howard becomes one of the Rangers who hunts him down. And the bandit's character, as delineated in the numerous stories that Cunningham gathers, conforms exactly to Joaquín's literary persona: he is courtly, elegant, melancholy and romantic, returning stolen items to pretty ladies and fighting duels for honor. Other literary motifs, such as the friendship between Love and Murieta, are repeated, and colorful characters typical of Gold Rush lore make their appearance. There's a mystery blonde with a Southern accent named "Old Nell," and Count de Boujacque, or Count the Bootjack, a.k.a. Count de Bunk and Doc the Bootjack, who claims to have once set Murieta's broken leg. A nickname like "Count de Bunk" apparently didn't raise Cunningham's suspicions in the slightest.

Even Frank Latta, himself a later and equally credulous collector of oral Murieta lore, was uncomfortable with Cunningham's book. Latta interviewed Cunningham's son and daughter, who told him that the book's publisher, hoping for a Hollywood contract, "rewrote the material in a flamboyant form." We also learn from Latta that Cunningham had a speech impediment, which may have hampered his conversations with sources, and that his original notes were accidentally burned by his mother, requiring him to rewrite his book from memory. All this casts serious doubt on the reliability of his information.

Meanwhile some historians were growing more dissatisfied with the acceptance of fables as historical fact. The greatest skeptic was Joseph Henry Jackson, whose *Bad Company,* first published in 1939, detailed the literary sources of much supposed Murieta history. Jackson believed Murieta to be a completely fictional character arising from two sources: the folk, because they need the "dashing outlaw" who steals from the rich and gives to the poor and who manifests a downtrodden people's "hidden defiances" and "private longings"; and Ridge's novel, which created "as preposterous a fiction as any the Dime Libraries ever invented," as Jackson would put it in his introduction to the 1955 reprint of Ridge's book.

Following Jackson, historians began to reject the beautified version of the criminal's life that had been validated by researchers like Bancroft and Hittell. Robert Glen Cleland's 1944 history of the state, *From Wilderness to Empire,* reduced Murieta to a "cutthroat Mexican bandit . . . out of whom tradition, romance, and the history-bedamned brand of motion picture have made a sort of bastard Robin Hood." Dismissed by the historians as a myth, a mere nostalgic stereotype like Zorro or the Cisco Kid, Murieta seemed destined to live on only in the fantasy worlds of popular literature and the folk legends of Mexicans and Gold Rush aficionados.

THIRTEEN

Joaquín was popular among Mexican readers on both sides of the border. But this Joaquín was an Anglo literary creation, only later made available to literate Mexicans. Was there an alternative Joaquín kept alive among traditions handed down by the folk?

Tracing the bandit's lore among the Mexican folk is tricky: most of the evidence is late and orally transmitted. The trouble is that the Murieta legend cannot be separated from Gold Rush folklore, in which he plays a major role; thus it is unclear whether the Murieta of song and legend reflects some long tradition of facts remembered by the people, or instead was constructed from prior literary incarnations. Moreover, folktales that tailored Joaquín to the outlaw formula were disseminated among California Anglos almost immediately after his death. Indeed, the earliest known folk-song about Murieta is one in English, "Joaquin the Horsethief," which circulated among Anglo miners.

The reminiscences of *vaquero* Arnoldo Rojas likewise exemplify the inherent difficulties of orally transmitted stories. Rojas tells the Murieta story—differing only in fine points from the literary version—as it was told to him forty years earlier in 1919 by an old *vaquero* nicknamed "Cartagena" after the city in Spain in which he was born. Cartagena told Rojas that there were "houses in Spain that owed their wealth to the good offices of Joaquín Murrieta." He then tells a story about Joaquín holding up some *gringo* thieves who themselves had just robbed some Spanish miners; Joaquín returns their money with a bonus taken from the *gringos.* Rojas later has the tale confirmed by another Spaniard in Mexico who tells basically the same story, with the hero announcing the famous tag *"Yo soy Joaquín,"*—"I am Joaquín"—which we have seen first entering the tradition from the *San Francisco Herald* newspaper story of April 18, 1853. The bandit's affection for Spaniards also has its origin in an earlier newspaper story (May 7, 1853) averring that the bandit never assaulted a Spaniard. Rojas's story itself is clearly a piece of folklore in the Robin Hood tradition, which already by 1919 had been established in numerous Anglo tales.

Other investigators over the years have collected fresh details relating to the Murieta legend, most gleaned from the tales of Gold Rush veterans and Murieta family members living in Sonora and elsewhere. Frank Latta, the amateur historian who wrote extensively about the San Joaquin Valley, spent thirty years tracking down anyone and everyone who could claim a connection to the bandit, apparently a population as large as that unearthed by James Cunningham. Latta interwove the material of these interviews with every bit of Murieta lore in circulation no matter what its origin, self-publishing the results of his labors in 1980. The result is a compendious, if somewhat disorganized, narrative, but unfortunately one whose factuality is impossible to determine.

According to Latta, Murieta was the leader of a group of "Horse Gangs" that ran mustangs and stolen horses from California to Mexico. Latta accepts the factuality of the rape (but not the murder) of

Murieta's wife and the lynching of his brother, along with his subsequent vengeance against the murderers. However, he denies that Murieta was killed at Cantua Creek. Instead, he asserts that the Rangers killed an Indian gang member named Chappo. There is a Chappo in the historical record, but he was in prison at the time of the battle. Murieta escaped, only to be mortally wounded in a gunbattle with authorities a few days later near Gilroy, south of San Jose. He was buried at his home on Alameda Creek in Niles Canyon near Oakland. Before he died, Murieta begged his wife not to let the *gringos* have the satisfaction of knowing they had killed him, which, we are asked to believe, is the reason why the story of his escape from Cantua Creek and his later death was kept secret by his wife.

This figment illustrates the illogic that frequently dogs Latta's book. Surely Rosita would know that the Rangers were displaying a head supposed to be her husband's, so there would be no point in keeping secret his death at the hands of *gringos*, since that was what everybody believed in any case. The only thing this story might explain is why Latta alone knew that Joaquín had been wounded near Gilroy and was buried in Niles Canyon.

As he recounts his tale, Latta provides a wealth of other fascinating but equally unverifiable circumstances. He tells us that the Rangers set out on their hunt with two five-gallon tin cans of alcohol in which they intended to preserve the heads, but drank it all before the gunfight. Latta also records an eyewitness description of the gunfight and Joaquín's escape by one Avelino Martínez, who claimed to be a gang member and who was interviewed by Latta at the age of one hundred. Latta regrettably transcribes this testimony into the broken English and mangled pronunciation of a stage Mexican: "Tres Dedos, maybe four 'ees men keel' [killed] een beeg fight weet' soldier, Arroyo Grande, maybe leave som'teen bury' [at] Las Tres Piedras." By remarkable coincidence, every detail of Martínez's story harmonizes with the information provided by Latta's many other informants.

But we cannot know finally whether the coherence of Latta's account results from its truth or from contrivance. Given the lack of independent corroboration by written documents, the most one can say of Latta's life work is that it is a valuable compendium of folklore and a testimony to the creative imagination of ordinary people.

Manuel Rojas is a Mexican historian who also interviewed Murieta family members in Sonora. He claims to have discovered the birth record of Joaquín—August 16, 1828—and another church record showing that Joaquín and Carmela Feliz stood godparents to a child on December 10, 1849. However, the name Carmela Feliz, a blending of Ridge's and the *Police Gazette*'s later names for Murieta's wife, is highly suspicious. Rojas also discovered through his interviews that Murieta, after the deaths of his wife and brother, formed an *acordada,* a secret pact, among twenty-two Californios and Mexicans. Their slogan was "All or nothing," which is also suspicious as this is the motto of the archetypal rebel in the essay by Albert Camus. They were organized into four troops, one of which was led by Joaquín Valenzuela, a veteran of Padre Jurata's guerillas during the Mexican War. The gang stole horses in order to finance a rebellion to recapture California for Mexico. Like Latta, Rojas does not believe Murieta was killed at Cantua Creek, asserting instead that he was at Los Angeles at the time and that it was Joaquín Valenzuela's head which was put on show. Hearing of the gun-battle, Murieta disbanded the group and returned to Mexico with his new wife, Ana Benitez, where he lived peacefully for another forty years.

Rojas's work ultimately suffers from the same limitations as Latta's and Cunningham's: the oral traditions cannot be shown to be independent of the literary creations that such traditions suspiciously resemble. Moreover, the length of time elapsed casts doubt on the reliability of their transmission from generation to generation. Understandably, Sonorans with the name Murrieta or those descended from that family, who have formed an organization called La Asociación Internacional Descendencia de Joaquín Murrieta, are eager to promote and contribute to a legend that glorifies one of their ancestors as a rebel against *gringo* aggression. As historian Thomas Gordon describes the process, "The legitimacy of the hero grows from this attachment and increasingly stimulates the folk to create further attachments."

Another important source of Murieta lore, especially for Mexicans, is the folksong. Again we face the same problem: given the difficulty of establishing priority, the folksong hero may be a descendant not of the real bandit as remembered by the folk, but of the literary character invented by Anglos for the entertainment of Anglos.

A form of folk ballad popular in the border regions of the Southwest is the *corrido,* a descendant of the Spanish *romance,* a popular song about the exploits of knights that accompanied the conquistadors to the New World. The *corrido* is usually built from verses consisting of four eight-syllable lines with the second and fourth lines rhyming, and takes as its subject events that are important to the community, giving prominence to the exploits of a hero. Though such songs were no doubt composed since the beginning of Mexican history, the *corrido* developed primarily in the mid-nineteenth century in the border region between Mexico and Texas, and reached its height in the period of the Mexican Revolution that began in 1910 with attacks against the dictatorship of Porfirio Díaz.

According to the historian Jose Limón, the border region was fertile ground for the *corrido:* "The concept of the local hero fighting for his right, his honor, and status against external foes, usually Anglo authorities, became the central theme of this balladry." So we might expect Murieta to be well represented in *corridos,* but only a few complete *corridos* and a few fragments about him exist, and these appear relatively late, suggesting that he was not a particularly admired figure among Mexicans beyond Sonora.

A *corrido* about Murieta was recorded in 1934 by the group Los Hermanos Sánchez y Limones, but it is impossible to know how far back the origins of this song go. In an interview years later, Victor Sanchez, one of the performers who recorded the song, said that he had heard it during the time of the Mexican Revolution. Concerning Murieta, Sanchez predictably said, "He robbed to give to the poor and the Indians. The *pueblo* [the people] thought of him as a Robin Hood."

The *corrido* itself clearly derives from the *Police Gazette* story, the same version that ended up in Spanish-language novels: Joaquín's wife is named Carmelita, a diminutive form of the *Police Gazette*'s Carmela, and she is killed. He is a noble defender of the weak: "The Indian poor and simple / I defended with fierceness," the ballad's Joaquín proclaims. Nowhere is there any evidence that the historical Murieta ever gave a thought to Indians, against whom his ancestors in Sonora had fought for centuries. But this elaboration of the Robin Hood motif—"From the greedy rich, / I took away their money"—obviously would appeal to dispossessed Indians fighting in the Revolution.

Also appealing to the politically weak would be the speaker's boasts about his twelve thousand victims, the terror he inspires in Americans (who tremble at his feet), and his Mexican nationality, for he takes pains to deny that he is Chilean. (This last detail perhaps reflects the popularity of the main Spanish-language literary version at the turn of the century, which made the bandit a Chilean.) This emphasis, and the speaker's claim that "From Mexico is California / because God wanted it that way," both likely reflect the nationalism and anti-Americanism rampant in northern Mexico during the revolution against Díaz, who was supported by the United States government and condemned for handing over Mexico's economy to foreigners.

In sum, this *corrido* demonstrates not the transmitted oral history of the folk, but rather the process by which a literary figure becomes a means for expressing political longings and vicarious vengeance—just as it had for John Rollin Ridge. The folktale elements just as likely derive from Anglo versions of the outlaw archetype as from stories of the Mexican people. Be that as it may, and whatever the origins of his legend, its survival among Californian Mexicans turned Joaquín into a powerful emblem of their own experiences and frustrations, one that a Mexican-American social movement of the sixties would return to a larger historical, social and political role.

FOURTEEN

The value of Joaquín as a symbol of power and retributive justice for the oppressed reemerged in the Chicano movement of the 1960's. "Chicano" is a word derived from *mejicano,* "Mexican," and in the early sixties it began to be used to designate Mexican-Americans by those activists and intellectuals who, inspired by the black consciousness movement, were trying to forge an ethnic identity in opposition to a mainstream American society regarded as racist and oppressive. The Chicano movement was in turn catalyzed by the farm workers' movement led by César Chávez.

By the 1960s Mexican immigrants, both legal and illegal, were numerically predominant among farmworkers in California, but this was a relatively late development. Prior to 1900 there was little economic incentive for Mexicans to make the journey to California through the harsh desert. The completion in 1927 of the railroad through northern Mexico to Los Angeles, the disruptive effect upon the peasants of the dictator Porfirio Díaz's regime and the resistance against it, and the development in California of labor-intensive crops like grapes and other fruit, along with refrigerated boxcars for shipment east, all created both a demand for cheap labor and a supply.

Initially the Chinese were the main source of farm labor, but the Chinese Exclusion Act of 1882 ended Chinese immigration. Japanese filled the void for a while, but the Immigration Act of 1924 reduced their numbers as well. Other groups—Hindustani, Armenians, Portuguese, Basques, Filipinos and others—were more numerous than Mexicans before World War I. The various laws restricting European immigration, however, made Mexicans a prime source of labor, starting in the Imperial Valley on the border. It is estimated that a million Mexicans crossed the border into the United States between 1900 and 1930. The economic crash of the Great Depression precipitated a repatriation movement that sent hundreds of thousands of Mexicans, including some United States citizens, back to Mexico. The *bracero* or guest worker program, which was started in 1942, allowed into the United States set numbers of Mexican workers, and along with other quotas further limited legal immigration. Illegal immigration, however, continued to provide California farms with cheap labor from Mexico.

The struggle to organize the farmworkers and the ensuing strikes and boycotts vaulted the Mexican farmworker and the Chicano into the national consciousness. The Chicano movement benefited from this publicity and from the increasing numbers of Mexican-Americans attending college in the sixties, where they were exposed to other ethnic identity movements and political theories. A key organization was the Crusade for Justice, an activist group led by Rodolfo "Corky" Gonzales, an ex-boxer and farmworker who became an important leader of the movement's more militant nationalistic wing. As described by Chicano historian Rodolfo Acuña, "the Crusade symbolized the struggle for control of the urban barrio, Chicano nationalism, and a Chicano identity that celebrated the Chicano nation of Aztlán." Aztlán is the mythical home of the ancient Aztecs, located generally in the Southwest or northern Mexico, but usually including California. The "Nation of Aztlán" came to embody the idealized national identity and reunification of the Mexican people who had been artificially divided by the Mexican War and the ceding of the Southwest to the United States. As such, Aztlán is the geographical equivalent of Murieta, a wish-fulfilling projection that compensates for the erosion of ethnic identity that occurs as more and more Mexicans assimilate into mainstream American culture.

According to the Chicano movement, not only had the Mexican national identity been wounded by the loss of California, but the land itself had been stolen from its rightful owners. The immigrant farmworkers and the inhabitants of the *barrios* are actually the true possessors of the land upon which they now toil or from which they are now excluded. Rodolfo Gonzales, in a speech given in Washington, D.C., in May 1968, articulated this historical injustice: "We opened our houses and hearts to him [the *gringo*] and trained him to irrigated farming, ranching, stock raising, and mining. He listened carefully and moved quickly, and when we turned around, he had driven us out and kept us out with violence, trickery, legal and court entanglements.... Robbed of our land, our people were driven to the migrant labor fields and the cities." In this mythic history, the huge Californio latifundia on which Indian peons worked for their Hispanic overlords and the fact that most Mexicans came to California during the twentieth century are both forgotten, not to mention the distinction between the prior Californios and the later immigrants.

One of the heroes used to dramatize the traumatic loss of California and the proper response to it was Joaquín Murieta, particularly in his guise as a rebel leader who organized resistance in order to wrest it away from the usurping gringos. A poem by "Corky" Gonzales, "I Am Joaquín: An Epic Poem," originally written in English, was distributed to striking farmworkers in California in 1966 and then published the next year. The poem has become probably the most famous piece of Chicano literature; it has sold over two hundred thousand copies in various editions and has been frequently anthologized; it has been made into a short film by Luis Valdez and produced as a play by many Chicano theatre troupes. According to historian Ignacio Garcia, the poem was used in Texas for recruiting young Mexicans into the movement, no doubt by firing them with righteous anger at the abuses heaped on a peaceful Mexican miner.

In Gonzales's poem, Murieta becomes the personification of the Chicano people and their national consciousness, their revolutionary heroes and their history—the last of these a record of unrelieved oppression, murder, land theft, rape, betrayal and revolution endured. Joaquín—ironically, from a historical perspective, since he was very likely not *mestizo*—is the representative of *la raza,* the Mexican *mestizo* "race," for his legend encapsulates the particular experience of the Mexican in California—"all men feared the guns of / Joaquín Murrieta. / I killed those men who dared / to steal my mine, / who raped and Killed / my love / my wife."

Consistent with the legend from its birth, Murieta is linked to the loss of land following the Mexican War: "My land is lost / and stolen, / My culture has been raped." The rapists are the gringos, "those hordes of Gold starved / Strangers / Who / changed our language / and plagiarized our deeds / as feats of valor / of their own." Rosita's rape now evokes the act of rape at the Conquest that created the Mexican people: the sexual and political submission of Malinche, the Aztec woman who was Cortez's interpreter and mistress, and whose name provides the noun *malinchista,* which denotes those corrupted by foreign influences. And this primal rape not only anticipates the rape of Joaquín's woman but also prefigures the "rape" of California and its Mexican culture by the new Anglo conquistadors and the Mexican collaborators who betray their own culture.

For Gonzales, Joaquín's function is relatively straightforward: he evokes the historical crime against the Mexican people that followed the annexation of California into the United States and consequently the need to resist assimilation into a sick, heartless Anglo culture. During the sixties, when some Mexican-Americans were recovering and creating a nationalist identity, a figure such as Joaquín was powerfully attractive, an emblem of Mexicans' legitimate claim to the land whose usurpers now despised them and exploited their labor. Moreover, Joaquín provided an object lesson in the futility of trying to assimilate to an alien and morally inferior culture, "to exist," Gonzales writes, "in the grasp / of American social neurosis, / sterilization of the soul / and a full stomach."

Equally attractive, to powerless farmworkers and college students alike, was the fantasy of retributive violence and the willingness to stand up for oneself that Murieta represented. In his history of Mexican-Americans, *La Raza,* Stan Steiner quotes from an article in the newspaper *La Raza* that praised assertive leaders like Rodolfo Gonzales: "Not since the days of Joaquín Murietta and Emiliano Zapata have the Mexican people ... had leaders they can be proud of." College students more likely to mimeograph manifestoes and occupy the dean's office than actually take up arms found a gratifying fantasy in violent heroes like Murieta, granted a new stature when conflated with historical revolutionaries like Zapata.

The sixties attraction toward "revolutionary violence" that made Murieta a symbol for the Chicano movement, when coupled with Marxist anti-Americanism, gave birth to another South American incarnation of the bandit. The Chilean Marxist poet Pablo Neruda's *Splendor and Death of Joaquín Murieta* is a play published in 1966 and frequently staged since then. Consistent with the Murieta tradition, Neruda's play is equal parts *Police Gazette* romance and crude leftist politics. In *Passions and Impressions* Neruda wrote that the play was "a long, romantic story flooded with brilliant color, though everything ends in the black of mourning." As for the politics, the figure of Murieta comes from "the tradition of Robin Hood"; the bandits "stole from the rich to give to the poor; that is, they returned to the plundered what they had taken from the plunderers." Ultimately, though, the politics of social banditry are subordinated to poetic self-actualization: "Perhaps," Neruda writes in the Foreword, "I undertook this song in the hope of losing myself for a time in the hazards of his lonely rebellion." Hence the long sentimental passages describing Joaquín's love for his wife.

This mythic self-expression with its lyric rhetoric is overlaid with anti-American clichés and Marxist bromides, all interspersed with frequent travelogue encomia to Chile. The Gold Rush and California, hawked in the play by "Tempters" in masks representing "Texans, Hooded Figures, etc.," clearly stand for the U.S. culture of materialist capitalism that corrupts the morally superior Third World: "All you Underdeveloped / Peoples—gold, there's nothing but gold!" What the Chileans actually find in America, of course, are racism and Texas Rangers who, accompanied by Klansmen, appear on stage in order to introduce a burlesque show that includes a golden stripper named Gold Louse and a character called the Gentleman Swindler, types of a decadent gringo culture driven by greed. Greed, in fact, is the American religion: the Klansmen, their hoods adorned with the faces of jackals and bloodhounds, perform a rite in which Gold is the Father and the Son, and Manifest Destiny is the Scripture. The Bloodhounds, as the Klansmen are now called, begin to scourge the miners and drive off what today we would call the "people of color."

After this, Neruda's story follows the *Police Gazette* scenario in which Murieta's wife, now a Chilena named Teresa, is raped and murdered, and the bandit wreaks his vengeance as "that implacable Horseman, the Avenger in search of / our birthright, our country, our race." Neruda leaves unexplained what "birthright" Chileans could possibly have in California. Murieta also champions the cause of the Indian who speaks to him of a "Great Spirit" and parrots the hoary platitudes of Noble Savage Indianism, such as "The earth is mother of us all." (This speech, by the way, is quoted by Neruda from Cossley-Batt's *Last of the California Rangers,* suggesting that its sentiments derive from American romanticism rather than Indian beliefs.) Scenes of redemptive bloodshed are depicted as the Bloodhounds' "Grand Wizard," who in reality is the "Gentleman Swindler," is killed by Joaquín.

Finally, the bandit is shot by one hundred cowardly "gringos with guns" who ambush him as he brings flowers to the grave of Teresa—the same final tableau favored by Hollywood in the film version of *The Robin Hood of El Dorado.* Neruda ends his play with a grotesque display of the bandit's severed head presented like a holy relic around which dance a chorus of chanting women, until the head itself speaks and announces that none other than Pablo Neruda will be the bandit's mouthpiece. As well as being a classic piece of sixties anti-American kitsch, Neruda's play is squarely in the bathetic tradition of Joaquín Miller and Marcus Stewart, in which revolutionary rhetoric attempts to redeem the sentimentalism.

Joaquín continues to be a popular icon for the Chicano and farmworker movements today. Very few "Chicanos" can be found outside university ethnic studies departments and classes, as most Mexicans in the real world are too busy working to raise their standard of living. In the privileged enclaves of the university, however, Murieta functions as a compensatory daydream of unjust victimization and retributive violence that is gratifying to professors with 401K pension funds and to law-abiding students who will become teachers and nurses. The United Farm Workers, a near nonentity in agricultural labor given the endless supply of eager workers from Mexico, also finds in Murieta an emblem of injustice punished that compensates for political and economic powerlessness. In 1968 a mural by Antonio Bernal at the United Farm Workers' Teatro Campesino Cultural Center in Del Rey, California, depicted Murieta alongside César Chávez: the hero of violent revenge paradoxically coupled with the hero of nonviolence. Likewise a poem in 1975 called "Nuestro Ideales" numbered Murieta among the heroes of the United Farm Workers, and the next year a version of the *corrido* recorded in the 1930s appeared in a songbook distributed to a UFW clinic in Delano. A critical difference between the two versions is the greater emphasis the latter puts on Murieta as a political liberator: "Now I'm leaving town; / We're all going to the fort / With a large enough cavalry / And a hundred thousand pesos." This discourse of revolutionary violence, of course, is a legacy of the sixties, a vestige of Romanticism disguised under a patina of banal theorizing from the works of Herbert Marcuse and Franz Fanon.

FIFTEEN

After the Chicano movement became institutionalized in university ethnic studies departments, Murieta took on a new life, half historical and half mythic. Many scholars were influenced by Marxist historian Eric Hobsbawm's 1969 theory of the "social bandit" who "challenges the economic, social and political order by challenging those who hold or lay claim to power, law, and the control of resources." The significance of these figures lies not in their historical truth, but in their power to represent and focus resistance to oppression: "We know," Hobsbawm writes, "that Joaquin Murieta of California is a literary invention; nevertheless, he is part of the structural study of banditry as a social phenomenon." Hobsbawm's thesis gave academic authority and political cachet to the long tradition of outlaw romance, and itself reflected the glorification of retributive violence popularized in films like *Bonnie and Clyde* (1967), which turned a pair of murderous psychopaths into glamorous Robin Hoods.

For some Chicano scholars, Hobsbawm's thesis was valuable inasmuch as it set aside the question of Murieta's historical existence. Writing in 1979, historian Gilberto López y Rivas wrote that Murieta combined "all of the traits of the archetypal social bandit." Murieta, "though he was but a literary fiction, might be taken as the true expression of the historical period." As in Gonzales's poem, what counted was not the bandit's objective existence but his power to represent, like Villa or Zapata, the Chicano nationalist identity and militant—one might even say macho—values. Joaquín is, as social historian Genaro Padilla puts it, a "composite name of Mexican social bandits."

Other works were not at all concerned with the question of historicity. *Furia y Muerte: Los Bandidos Chicanos,* published in 1973 under the auspices of the Chicano Studies Center at UCLA, makes no distinction between fiction and history in its retelling of the Murieta story. Ridge's and Paz's fictions are cited as historical sources, as are the works of historians like Mitchell and Hittell who were themselves dependent on Ridge's novel. Gold Rush popular history, most of it comprising little more than folktales, is mined as well for presumable facts. Despite the obligatory nod to the "social bandit" thesis, nowhere is the student tipped off that Murieta is a character of fiction rather than a historical person.

The treatment of Murieta by some Chicano academics reveals the politicization of intellectual work that followed the creation of university programs whose purpose is ethnic cheerleading and the massaging of self-esteem rather than the scholarly pursuit of truth. An anthology of Mexican-American literature called *Aztlán,* also published in 1973, seems completely oblivious to the distinction between fiction and history. In a section called "The Guerilla Wars," Murieta is depicted as leader of a "revolution" supported by the "dons of the old families of California." The only documentary source is that old fabulist Major Horace Bell, the Los Angeles Ranger whose memoirs are notorious for their unreliability. A manifesto called "I Will Not Submit" is published; its source is Walter Noble Burns's novel *The Robin Hood of Eldorado*! Some folklore by the *vaquero* Arnoldo Rojas is recycled, and the whole section ends with something called "Love Secrets of Joaquin Murieta," from an "undated and unidentified newspaper" unearthed in 1969. This Joaquín is straight out of central casting, serenading his cousin-lover with the guitar while the posse is hot on his heels.

A survey of a few textbooks popular in Chicano studies courses reveals a distinction between scholars who acknowledge that Murieta is a legend, albeit one of representative significance, and those who apparently believe the legend is factually true. Meier and Ribera's *Mexican Americans/American Mexicans* states that the bandit is "largely legendary." Other less careful scholars accept the "social bandit" description but apply it to a person they consider a historical figure. Historian Alfredo Mirandé numbers Murieta among the "Mexican social bandits" who "challenged the dominant order," and accepts the historicity of the fictions created by Ridge, whom he cites as a bona fide source. So too does James Diego Vigil in *From Indians to Chicanos*. His bibliography lists Ridge under a 1969 reprint; an unsuspecting student could not know that the work is a dime novel actually published in 1854.

Rodolfo Acuña's *Occupied America*, a textbook in its fourth edition, is ambiguous when it comes to the historical reality of Murieta. Calling the bandit "legendary" or a "legend in his times" doesn't clarify his status, since a real person can become a legend. Acuña at least uses the adverb "supposedly" when mentioning the cause of Murieta's turn to banditry—the rape and death of his wife. As we have seen, having Rosita (or Carmela) raped *and* killed is a sure sign of *Police Gazette* origins. Acuña, however, doesn't even get the myth right, having Joaquín track down and kill the "man" rather than the several men responsible for Rosita's death. Whether myth or history, though, Murieta's value ultimately lies in his recourse to murderous violence—or "antisocial behavior," as Acuña euphemizes it—justifiably directed against usurping oppressors.

The typical strategy of some Chicano historians today is to place statements implying that Murieta is a real person alongside others that set aside the question of objectivity as unimportant. A recent study called *Border Visions* claims Murieta as the "leader of the first rebellion in California" who "organized resistance with an alternative 'auxiliary' political authority and general community approval and legitimacy for his actions." These sound like statements of historical fact, but on the next page the author asserts that Murieta is a "hero to be cherished regardless of the reality of the man" or his actions. The reproduction of the spurious Marshall photograph should give the reader pause, as should the statement at the book's end that the author has "told the tale without the pretence of being 'objective.' "

San Diego State Chicano studies professor Richard Griswald del Castillo, who has written an introduction to a recent reprint of Walter Noble Burns's novel, is more forthright about what he calls "the problematic relationship between history and myth"—before going on to tell essentially the Ridge/*Police Gazette* version of Murieta's life and actions, with additional "facts" provided by historians of Murieta family lore like Mexican historian Manuel Rojas. To his credit, del Castillo does admit, concerning the lynching of Murieta's brother and the rape and killing of his wife, that "no documents verify these specific injustices." His conclusion is the standard one that many modern historians endorse: "The problem is to decide for ourselves which incarnation of Murieta's life helps us make the most sense of our contemporary life." History is not the record of real people and their actions, but a fable whose value lies in its therapeutic or political efficacy. We are back to John Rollin Ridge and the novel he wrote to help make sense of his own life and experiences.

Outside of Chicano studies departments, most academic historians today consider Joaquín to be largely a legendary figure, though one who represents various aspects of the clash between Americans and Mexicans in Gold Rush California. A standard textbook of California history by James J. Rawls and Walton Bean, *California: An Interpretive History,* now in its seventh edition, discusses the "vague and dubious factual background" of the bandit in the context of Gold Rush literary history and writers like John Rollin Ridge and Joaquín Miller. A recent study of racial conflict in California history, *Five Fires,* says that "the persecution of immigrants from Mexico and points south generated a powerful myth of reaction." In the Joaquín of Ridge's novel, "Californians of all races joined together to create a fable of payback." Author David Wyatt concludes that "the fragility of the evidence anticipates the eclipse of fact by legend [as] the story of Murieta began to displace the events that had given it meaning." Likewise, Steven Schwartz, in his recent study of California, *From West to East,* calls Joaquín's story "a heroic myth of Spanish resistance"; his importance lies in his ability to "embod[y] both the ambivalence felt by Americans occupying the land and the real impoverishment and other oppression felt by the Hispanic population in American California."

Less careful historians do not make it clear that Murieta is mostly a fictional character. The authors of *The American West*—who warn us that they eschew being "completely objective"—number Murieta among the "social bandits" who "robb[ed] from the rich to provide for the poor." The reader is left with the impression that Joaquín did likewise, which of course he didn't. This carelessness continues throughout the discussion, despite the loophole of calling the bandit "semifictional," since the authors don't specify which half is fiction and which is history. Thus the authors call Ridge's work "an important book" instead of making clear that it was a dime novel, and they claim that the *corrido* about Murieta was sung "for the next half-century" after his death, although the earliest evidence for a ballad about him dates from the early twentieth century. And to speak of "Murrieta's accomplishments" is disingenuous to say the least, given that one of the few certain facts we do have is that those accomplishments included slitting the throats of innocent Chinese.

Scholars influenced by postmodernist and multiculturalist approaches to history have also discovered a fertile field in the Murieta legend. Postmodernist history, as defined by historian Gertrude Himmelfarb, is "a denial of the fixity of the past, of the reality of the past apart from what the historian chooses to make of it, and thus of any objective truth about the past." We have seen this approach applied to Joaquín in the work of those Chicano historians who are willing to set aside or fudge the question of objectivity. Postmodernist relativism thus undergirds multiculturalist history, which focuses on the oppression and exclusion of minorities on the part of a dominant white society that shapes history to serve its own pretensions to superiority. The issues of historical truth are sidestepped, since multiculturalist history serves a greater liberationist goal: raising the consciousness of excluded and oppressed minorities through the restoration of their authentic identity and their distorted and hidden history and heroes.

Susan Lee Johnson takes this approach in her study of social conditions during the Gold Rush. Johnson's aim is "to interrogate and to dismantle the stories white Americans have told themselves" about the Gold Rush. These stories, she claims, justify and encode white male dominance and exclusion of the "other"; they are the "first step in the long discursive process by which whole pieces of [the Gold Rush] past fell by the wayside of history." Johnson is frank about the liberationist aims that inform her presumably scholarly history: the "social movements" concerned with race, class, sexuality and gender "have most deeply influenced [her] thinking in this book" which "openly yearns for social relations in which difference and domination are not so closely, so predictably, and so devastatingly linked to one another."

Johnson starts her book with Murieta's story, as it is representative of that whole exclusionary process; whether or not it is true is beside the point, though she implies throughout that what she is telling us about the bandit is factual. Yet her reconstruction of the story is dependent on the highly unreliable oral folklore gathered by Frank Latta, which in turn has its ultimate source in Ridge's dime novel and the *Police Gazette*. Johnson's indifference to historicity leads to statements patently false, as when she says, regarding Murieta's pursuit by the Rangers, that "a Mexican family [*sic!*] fled from a well-armed, state-sponsored band of Anglo Rangers" who, incited by rumors of "*alleged* banditry," typified "Anglos' hysterical response to *perceived* brigands" (my emphases). In Johnson's telling, it is the numerous documented Chinese, Mexican and Anglo victims of the bandit and his gangs, not to mention other circumstances such as Murieta's blond hair and blue eyes, that "fall by the wayside of history." The yearning for social relations free of "dominance and difference" can apparently justify a multitude of historiographical sins.

Timothy Powell's study of Ridge's novel offers a more nuanced interpretation of the bandit, at least in his literary incarnation. Powell correctly sees that the "dualistic critical vision that bifurcates the multicultural novel into the overly simplistic theoretical categories of oppressor and oppressed" is too crude for getting at the significance of Joaquín, for it obscures "the intricate cultural complexities of 'American' identity."

Thus the collapsing of oppressed Indian and oppressed Mexican into one category that is then contrasted with the Anglo oppressor ignores many details that defy this dualism. For example, Ridge was a half-white Southern sympathizer and slave-owner who looked down on the Indians he considered less civilized than the Cherokee, and whose rage was directed not against the white oppressors whom he counseled Indians to emulate, but against the Cherokee faction that murdered his father. In the novel too, Murieta's victims are more frequently the Chinese who were more marginalized and oppressed than were Joaquín and his fellow gang members. In Powell's interpretation, these conflicts and complexities must be taken into account in order more accurately to delineate the "complicated cultural hybridity of 'American' identity that is forged in the midst of contentious and racist forces of cultural exclusion in nineteenth-century California."

Powell's vision of a contentious "cultural hybridity" is more historically accurate than the essentialist melodrama of better-known multicultural theory. Unfortunately, his shaky grasp of California history leads him to make statements reflecting the "binarism" he is trying to escape, and blinds him to factors that actually strengthen his argument for interethnic complexity.

For example, Powell's anachronistic use of "Mexican American" obscures the contentious cultural and even ethnic differences between Californios and Mexican immigrants. His take on the land grant disputes—the standard "gringos-stole-our-land" interpretation—ignores the fact that latifundia owned by *ranchero* grandees were worked by Indian serfs, and that Californio *ricos* on occasion identified more closely with rich Anglos than with *cholo* Mexicans. Nor does he note that many Latin American miners worked claims with peon labor, or that many Americans protested the Foreign Miners Tax not just because they were losing business but because they recognized that it was unfair. Powell's most important omission, however, is his failure to acknowledge that there is strong evidence that the historical Murieta was probably fair-haired and blue-eyed. This fact more than anything else turns the essentialist notions of ethnic identity that Powell rightly criticizes, but seemingly cannot escape, into a crude simplification of the "contradictory and conflicted complexity" of American identity.

SIXTEEN

Joaquín's bottled head, whatever it looked like and whoever once looked out from its eyes, has its own history as convoluted as the stories that have sprung up concerning its suggested owner. Indeed, the morbid fascination for his severed head may account for much of the interest Joaquín has aroused over the years, for it is a most graphic evocation of the barbarity and crude justice one associates with his times.

The head and Three-Fingered Jack's hand toured the Gold Country towns the summer of Joaquín's death, and numerous people either confirmed or challenged the head's identity. Tales immediately began to circulate about the horrid trophies. As is usual in such cases, it was put about that Joaquín's hair and Jack's three fingernails continued to grow. One legend has a stagecoach from Sonora held up because it was thought to be transporting the priceless head. Latta tells another story, relayed to him by Hank and George Hawn, about a crowd at Diamond Springs who threatened to hurl the head into the street because it wasn't Joaquín's.

After leaving the gold country, the head was exhibited in Stockton, and from there it went to San Francisco. An advertisement in the *Herald* of August 18, 1853, announced that for the sum of one dollar, "Joaquin's Head!!" could be viewed at John King's Saloon on Sansome Street. The *Golden Era*'s Rollin Daggett snorted, "We question whether the living bandit robbed our citizens of more money than have those who are exhibiting his *dead head*."

The next year, Ranger John Chiles was showing the head in San Francisco. He claimed in print that this was the only way Harry Love and the Rangers could recoup the money they had spent in tracking and capturing the bandits. Not long after this, the head and hand dropped out of sight. One story has both mementos stolen. In 1855 the sheriff of San Francisco County seized the head from a man named Wothring for nonpayment of debt. The head sold at auction for $36 to J. V. Plume and Judge Lyons, who quickly made a profit by selling it the next day for $100 to Andrew J. Taylor, also known as "Natchez" after the Mississippi town of his birth. Natchez owned a gun shop and shooting gallery on Clay Street. The auction generated its own legend: When Sheriff Harrison dropped the gavel on the sale, an Irishman cried out, "Oh! Is it possible that you are going to sell the head of your fellow-creature!" and predicted bad luck for both seller and buyer.

In one tale, the Irishman's prediction comes true: the sheriff accidentally shoots himself. Actually, it was Natchez who later shot himself while examining a pistol; the sheriff is thought to have committed suicide. Natchez was famous for providing the pistols used in the many duels fought during Gold Rush years. According to Horace Bell, Natchez had supplied the pistols used in the famous 1859 duel between David C. Broderick, an Irish stonemason who became a U.S. senator, and state supreme court judge David S. Terry, a Southerner outraged by Broderick's stand against slavery in the Senate. Natchez was rumored to have secretly set the triggers with extreme delicacy so that the guns would fire when raised, and to have whispered to Terry just before the duel. Broderick accidentally fired his first shot into the ground when he raised his pistol too quickly, and Terry then killed him. Bell, by the way, discounts the slander, since Terry was "the soul of honorable chivalry." The pistol that Natchez was showing when it discharged, thus fulfilling the curse of Murieta's head, was said to be the very same pistol that Terry had used to shoot Broderick: again that folkloric delight in juxtaposing notorious figures!

Bell also recounts a ghost story associated with the severed head. Henderson told Bell that "there was not a day, or more usually a night, that Joaquín did not come to him personally, headless, and speak—for his voice was recognizable even though his head was missing." The bandit announced, "I am Joaquín and I want my head back," and the brave Henderson rationally replied that he was "powerless to restore it" but had "always been sorry that I did cut it off." This same story was told about Byrnes, who allegedly was driven to drink and insanity by the hectoring apparition.

According to the *San Joaquin Republican* of February 1856, a certain Mr. Craigmiles was the next owner of the head, and he had dreams of making $50,000 exhibiting the relic in a tour "of the Atlantic states," starting in New Orleans and ending in New York.

But the tour never happened, and a few months later the head was sold to someone who, as a newspaper item comically put it, "was silly enough to give eleven dollars for the bijou."

It was not until 1865 that the head reached its final home at Dr. Jordan's Pacific Museum of Anatomy and Science on Market Street, San Francisco. Dr. Jordan's establishment displayed oddities such as a four-legged chicken, a kangaroo in spirits, Egyptian mummies, various body parts of infamous criminals and something called the Cyclops Child. Dr. Jordan was the author of several books, including one called *The Philosophy of Marriage*— "illustrated with cases"— and others describing the horrors of masturbation. He included in his exhibitions life-sized painted wax figures illustrating in gruesome detail the ravages of venereal disease. Apparently some people thought these works were virtual pornography, since Dr. Jordan at one point was charged with maintaining an immoral exhibition.

Dr. Jordan seems to have run another interesting racket. According to one Tom Wauhab, who had visited the museum, patrons viewing his horrifying wax figures would sometimes start imagining that they suffered from the same diseases and, in Wauhab's words as reported by Frank Latta, "then there was a half dozen so-called doctors waitin' t'pounce on yuh. You imagined yuh had every disease in the place an' them doctors helped you along." Latta himself visited the museum with a friend in 1906, the August after the earthquake. While they were there, he saw two men collapse and be carried into a back room for "treatment." Describing the "Pathological Room" of wax figures, Latta says "it was so real we could smell it." He and his friend bolted immediately.

Most historians report that the museum and head were both destroyed in the earthquake. According to the eyewitness Charles Bull, who claimed he was near the museum right after the quake and before the fires consumed it, "All was a shambles. Shelves were emptied into aisles and everything breakable was smashed. The great bowl had been shattered and lying on its ear among the fragments was the gruesome head of Murrieta." This testimony obviously contradicts Latta's claim that he visited the museum after the earthquake. In fact, by 1906 Jordan's museum had moved to McAllister Street, and its building wasn't burned, so Bull was either fabricating or misremembering. Latta's story is full of holes as well, since the specimens and exhibits he and his chum went to see would have been damaged even if the building didn't burn, as his own research testifies.

By 1929, when Latta made another visit, the museum had closed. Latta did track down a janitor who had worked there at the time of the quake. According to his testimony, when he entered the premises six weeks after the earthquake, all the jars of specimens had been shaken off their shelves and smashed. Any specimens that could not be saved were buried in the alley. As the janitor pointed to the spot of interment, Latta "looked at the alley pavement; concrete, probably ten inches thick. On one side was a multi-storied building. On the other side was a building with concrete walls set on a concrete foundation." And presumably that is where, to this day, the head of the famous bandit rests, beneath tons of concrete, alongside the spoiled freaks and oddities of Dr. Jordan's museum.

But that is not the end of the persistent memento's fascination. In the 1970s a man named Walter Johnson in Santa Rosa claimed to have the head, which he stored in a vault; historian Hector Lee published a photograph of it in a 1987 article. The head resembles the sketch made in 1895, allegedly while the head was on display in Dr. Jordan's museum. Johnson's head supposedly surfaced in 1957, when an old man's property was disposed of at his death (a story suspiciously similar to the one Bell tells about his portrait of Joaquín). In another version, the old man's house was near Jordan's museum in San Francisco and he rescued the head from the ruins. From there the head went to the Old Town Museum in New Almaden south of San Jose, and at some point a man named Al Keck acquired it in a bankruptcy sale—the second time the head was disposed of at auction. Keck sold it to Johnson for a horse, a Jeep and a gun worth $1,600, along with a letter from a man who claimed that this was the head he had seen in Jordan's museum before 1906.

In 1976 a reporter for the *San Jose Mercury News* tracked down the head's origin. A woman who ran a museum near the Old Town Museum, which was owned by a man named Frank Dean, told the reporter, "Frank Dean had it [the head] made by a wax museum. It's nothing but wax and human hair stuck into it." The reporter offered to x-ray the head, but Johnson declined: "If it's a fake I don't want to know it"—a fitting motto for the Murieta legend itself.

Meanwhile, folklore surrounding the head continued to proliferate. *Vaquero* Arnoldo Rojas claimed that Murieta had escaped to Sonora and lived out his days "with bitter memories" in the town of Cucurpe. After he died, however, the *gringos* learned of his death and burial. "Still in keeping with their earlier acts of barbarism, they denied him, to the very last, the right to human dignity. They committed the last indignity by an act of desecration of the dead. They dug up his bones to measure his cranium!" Presumably that's how the bandit's head ended up in Jordan's museum and then Johnson's vault.

According to another story, the head and Three-Fingered Jack's hand exercised occult powers. In 1980 Sig Christopherson, one of the original organizers of the Murrieta Horsemen's Pilgrimage, claimed that a fire the previous year in the building occupying the Market Street site of Jordan's museum, "assorted odd" happenings in Fresno County, and the 1906 earthquake itself were all caused by the "desperate attempt of the two men's severed parts to rejoin their interred bodies." To forestall any more such disasters, a Father McAllister blessed the building, and dirt and rubble from the site were taken to Three Rocks and buried. No one seemed to be aware that at the time of the 1906 earthquake, Jordan's museum no longer occupied the Market Street site.

California writer Richard Rodriguez, in one of the best essays on the ambivalent meaning and attraction of Murieta, tells of visiting the head owned by Johnson in Santa Rosa. Rodriguez grew up hearing spooky tales about Murieta from his grandmother, but he learned of the head from a Jesuit professor at the University of San Francisco, Alberto Huerta, who has written several articles about Murieta. Huerta showed Rodriguez a copy of a letter he had sent to Governor George Deukmejian, requesting the state's help in finding the bandit's head so that it could be given a suitable burial as a "symbolic act of reconciliation." Father Huerta imagined a funeral mass at Mission Santa Clara, with *corridos* composed and sung by Joan Baez.

As Huerta tries to recruit Rodriguez to his cause, they visit Sig Christopherson, the "Mexican Sigui," the same Sig who had the building blessed in San Francisco and long agitated on behalf of Murieta's memory. He persistently lobbied the state legislature to buy the land around Arroyo Cantua, exonerate Murieta and remove the historical marker because it refers to him as "the notorious bandit." He would point out ominously that the epicenter of the 1983 Coalinga earthquake was directly beneath the marker. Christopherson was a font of Murieta lore, telling of accidents caused on Highway 152 as it winds through Pacheco Pass by drivers swerving to avoid horsemen materializing out of the fog. (Since the highway was widened, the number of accidents has decreased substantially.) Christopherson also told of sitting with some drinking buddies outside a locked bar early one morning in the 1970s, when they all heard Mexican guitars from inside the cantina and saw candles flickering behind the curtains.

Having learned of Johnson's relic, Huerta and Rodriguez drive to Santa Rosa and finally get to see it. Johnson's son Bill explains to them that the suspicious-looking crack on the lip is from the mortician's clay that was spread over the head to preserve it. The eyes are open, and Bill says an undertaker told him that the eyes showed the man had died a violent death. He doesn't respond to Huerta's offer to take the head off his hands. As they drive south back to San Francisco, Huerta comments, "Did you notice? The head is expanding. I think it's going to explode." Rodriguez muses, "I imagine the explosion of the hideous piñata rocking the mission church at Santa Clara. The governor. 'Dies Irae.' Joan Baez. Sombreros in the air." Just before the Golden Gate Bridge, Huerta says, "Somebody should bury that thing."

Rodriguez's delicate irony and humor beautifully capture the powerful allure and vague creepiness of the head. The legend of Joaquín appears by essay's end to be a romantic illusion from the past that deflects people's attention from the very different late-twentieth-century California in which they now must live and navigate politically. The head and the legend ultimately embody the fantasy history and compensatory yearnings of many Mexican-Americans and many Anglos as well.

But legends die hard, and history is notoriously difficult to pin down. We still don't know for sure who was gunned down at Cantua Creek that July Sunday in 1853, or whose severed head actually toured the gold country before finding a home in Dr. Jordan's waxworks. Perhaps the head sitting on Walter Johnson's kitchen table could have been made to speak through modern forensic analysis, revealing itself to be the "right Joaquín, and no mistake," as Harry Love claimed, or a waxen fake like most of the legend itself. But like that other head that may be resting beneath tons of San Francisco concrete, Walter Johnson's Joaquín is lost forever. According to his granddaughter, Johnson, tired of being pestered by the health department about keeping human remains, buried the head in a secret location.

THE RIDE BACK TO THREE ROCKS

About 160 miles northeast of Three Rocks the old Gold Rush town of Coulterville sits on Highway 49 among the oaks of the Sierra foothills, between Sonora to the north and Hornitos to the south, both towns rich in Gold Rush and Murieta lore. Coulterville started off as a Mexican mining settlement called Banderita or "Little Flag," and in the heyday of the Gold Rush had a population of five thousand Mexicans, Americans, Chinese and French. Today barely more than one hundred people live among the still preserved Gold Rush era buildings such as the Sun Sun Wo store, still containing its original shelves and counters, or the Hotel Jeffrey, which once had a Mexican *fandango* on its second floor. Another attraction from those days is the hanging tree, a gnarled oak from which sixty miscreants are said to have been hanged.

Sitting as it does in the midst of Gold Rush country in Mariposa County, it's not surprising that in September, Coulterville celebrates Joaquín Murrieta Days, an occasion for connecting civic pride to the Gold Rush past. On Saturday morning a parade marches through town, featuring a high school marching band, a rodeo queen, mounted representatives of various organizations such as the U.S. Marshals and the Veterans of Foreign Wars, a miniature horse named Rambo pulling a carriage, and actors costumed as Gold Rush era miners, gamblers, ruffians and "ladies of the night," with a few gun-battles thrown in. Nearby are booths selling food, quilts, Indian jewelry and a book that condenses Frank Latta's research on Murieta.

In the afternoon the legend of Murieta itself takes center stage in a play acted out on the porch of the post office. The Coulterville drama follows the Romantic version of Joaquín's career created by

John Rollin Ridge. The whipping of Joaquín, the death of his brother, the rape and murder of Rosita are all dramatized, overlaid with a narrative placing the events in the context of the Foreign Miners Tax and anti-immigrant prejudice on the part of drunken boors. After suffering these outrages, Joaquín recruits his gang with the announcement that it is "time to defend our rights," relating personal injury to the larger question of California's troubled integration into the United States.

For most Anglos who know about him, Joaquín remains an archetypal outlaw who was driven to crime by injustice and whose deeds are memorialized in songs like "The Ballad of Joaquín Murrieta," by Jack Hannah of the folk-singing group Sons of the San Joaquin, and in the folk history and tourist hype of just about every Gold Rush town, most of which can display a secret tunnel or bullet-pocked wall associated with the famous badman. California history has become a commodity, as it did at the end of the nineteenth century when the Gold Rush and Murieta, *rancho* and mission all became part of a marketable myth that gave new Californians a sense of place and continuity with the past.

The Coulterville festival features this incarnation of Joaquín, the glamorous but bloodthirsty bandit evocative of those wilder and perhaps more interesting days of California's raucous, disorderly youth, which now can be left behind—safely and agreeably regretted. This is the Romantic Joaquín.

The annual ride of the Joaquín Murieta Horseman's Pilgrimage that ends at Cantua Creek on the last Sunday morning of July highlights the other vision of the bandit, the victim of racist oppression who seeks justice. This is Joaquín the Avenger.

The crucial difference between these two aspects lies in how they are received outside the communities that host the celebrations. Thus the Three Rocks Joaquín—as much the invention of Ridge and Anglo writers as the other—is frequently taken as an authentic figure whose sufferings and justified response imply a timeless paradigm for contemporary Mexican-Americans, one that provides a historical warrant for political redress in the present.

The local media coverage of the event is usually an occasion for the recycling as history of much Murieta folklore that has accumulated over the years, frequently in the service of ethnic cheerleading and grievance politics. Typical is the coverage in the *Fresno Bee,* the largest newspaper in central California. Participants speak of honoring Murieta's "contributions" or "spirit"; the rape of Murieta's wife and the hanging of his brother are reported as history; and other historically undocumented information is presented as fact, such as the claim that while he was alive Murieta became a folk hero and was known as the "Mexican Robin Hood"—in reality a pure figment of Anglo fabulists. A columnist for the *Bee* observes that the ride itself started in order to recognize Murieta "as a man of justice and peace," and always there are the obligatory references to the "stolen land," without any apparent awareness that the "land" in reality consisted of vast estates worked by the Indians from whom it had been appropriated. At least this time the paper doesn't print the make-believe Marshall photograph, as it did the previous year.

Murieta's historical existence is clearly not as important as his representative value, particularly for political activists who find compliant allies in a media deferent to multicultural identity politics. The annual ride itself started not as the spontaneous expression of the folk eager to recognize one of their heroes and recover his lost history, but partly as a way for a Madera County supervisor to call attention to migrant workers in the Three Rocks area who were being forced from their homes for health code violations.

But always the political is entangled with the personal. Another organizer was "Mexican Sigui," that same Sig Christopherson who believed that Murieta's unburied head and sullied reputation were causing earthquakes and other mischief in California. Christopherson's interest in Murieta flowed from his personal affection for the Mexican people, and he helped organize the pilgrimage out of gratitude after several Mexican friends had donated blood when he needed it for an operation. This blending of the personal and political has defined the bandit's legend from the start, especially in John Rollin Ridge's novel, where Joaquín's experience is a projection of the novelist's anger against the murderers of his father.

The media's coverage of the ride is consistent with the academics' exploitation of Joaquín. Chicano scholars and activists, most of whom these days reside in universities, find in Joaquín a convenient symbol of identity-politics grievances and the persistent racism of a dominant Anglo culture that swiped California from its rightful owners. This interpretation of history is simplistic and reductive, ignoring as it does the remarkable variety covered by labels such as "Hispanic" or even "Mexican."

A better use of the bandit's legend would instead illustrate that variety. For just as the mysterious Joaquín appears at various times as a *mestizo,* an Indian or a fair-haired *güero,* so too one can find today in California light-skinned Mexican boys named Josh who ride skateboards and are into punk music; Indian farmworkers with profiles right off a Mayan glyph who can't speak Spanish and are looked down upon by Mexican-American clerks at Wal-Mart; and fourth-generation, college-educated soccer moms of Mexican descent who barely speak Spanish, if at all, and who have married Anglos. If the myth of Joaquín has any relevance beyond outlaw romance or Gold Rush entertainment, it comes not from his status as an icon of multicultural victim-politics, but from the way his legend expresses the great drama of immigration and assimilation, the complex collision and blending of cultures experienced by every ethnic group that has made its way to America.

I suspect that for most of the Mexicans who gather at Our Lady of Lourdes Mission Church in Three Rocks every July, Joaquín's value indeed lies in embodying the plight of Mexican immigrants, rather than in memorializing the historical injustice visited upon the Californios or in providing an iconography of imagined revolution for well-heeled academics. For most of the riders Murieta is simply an immigrant who came to pursue economic opportunities but instead encountered, as have many immigrants to America, discrimination and prejudice. That reading of the bandit makes sense, considering that most of the Mexicans in the Valley immigrated after World War II and have little or no connection to the California of the Gold Rush, let alone to the feudal land barons of Alta California. Certainly in my own experience most Mexicans, whether immigrants or American-born, are simply pursuing the American dream, too interested in improving their lives and their children's lives to dream of reconquering the mythic homeland of Aztlán or returning California to a Mexico that many of them risked their lives to leave.

The search for Joaquín, then, finds many Joaquíns, each playing a role shaped by our desires: the avenging rebel against *gringo* tyranny; the doomed lover who evokes the exotic strains of Old California; the chivalrous outlaw ever ready to defend his honor; and the emblem of all the adventure and excitement of the Gold Rush. He conjures for us an elemental, colorful world where life is lived more intensely and passionately, and where sword, knife or pistol settles justice quickly and definitively.

And so powerful is the attraction of this world, so superior is its myth to our grubby world of complexity and compromise and muddled aims, that it has been made real, like Pygmalion's statue, by the force of our wishes. But no matter how appealing it is, I believe we should resist this colonizing of history, this confusion between the imagined and the real, this temptation to "print the legend."

After all, it is commitment to psychologically satisfying myths that drove much of the slaughter of the past century. No matter how difficult to uncover, no matter how uncertain and complex—or displeasing and unwelcome—our historical truths, I believe we must still diligently and modestly search for the truth of affairs and resist the simplifications, the selectivity of myths and legends. However attractive we may find some aspect of Joaquín, however satisfying and fulfilling, we must remember what he undeniably left behind him: the slit throats and bullet-riddled chests of his victims.

NOTES

The reader will notice three ways of spelling the bandit's surname. "Murieta" is the spelling that was used by John Rollin Ridge and that I have used. Modern-day Sonorans spell the name "Murrieta." "Murietta" is incorrect, since Spanish does not double the "t" as does Italian.

The Feliz-Murieta Spree

page

9ff. Feliz and Murieta gang crimes: Boessenecker, *Gold Dust and Gunsmoke,* 73–99; Varley, *The Legend of Joaquín Murrieta,* 15–65. Latta, *Joaquín Murietta and His Horse Gangs,* 36–75, reproduces many of the newspaper stories reporting the crimes from 1853.

10 Sonora: in Johnson, *Roaring Camp,* 59–62.

12 *San Francisco Herald:* In Varley, *The Legend of Joaquín Murrieta,* 25.

13 Harry Love: Varley, *The Legend of Joaquín Murrieta,* 28–30.

17 Clarke interview: in Boessenecker, *Gold Dust and Gunsmoke,* 91.

17–18 Newspaper reports: in Latta, *Joaquín Murrieta and His Horse Gangs,* 38.

19 Newspaper reports: in Latta, *Joaquín Murrieta and His Horse Gangs,* 45, 49.

20 San Luis Obispo crimes: in Nadeau, *The Real Joaquín Murieta,* 75.

20–21 Love's later life: in Nadeau, *The Real Joaquín Murieta,* 110–11.

21 *Los Angeles Star:* in Varley, *The Legend of Joaquín Murrieta,* 97.

23f. Newspaper reports: Varley, *The Legend of Joaquín Murrieta,* 104.

23–24 *San Francisco Alta California:* in Varley, *The Legend of Joaquín Murrieta,* 67.

24 *Stockton Journal:* Nadeau, *The Real Joaquín Murieta,* 99.

24 Ben Bolt: in William B. Secrest, "Horrifying History of a Highwayman's Head," 47–50.

24 Ochoa: Varley, *The Legend of Joaquín Murrieta,* 173.

24 *Daily Herald* letter: Secrest, *The Return of Joaquin,* 9.
25 *Alta* again: Varley, *The Legend of Joaquín Murrieta,* 119.
25 *San Francisco Chronicle:* Nadeau, *The Real Joaquín Murieta,* 103.
26 Rosie Martinez: in Romero, *Joaquin Murrieta,* 25.
26 Description of Joaquín Carillo: *San Joaquin Republican,* 16 February 1853.
26 Gov. Bigler's reward proclamation reproduced in Latta, *Joaquín Murrieta and His Horse Gangs,* 321.
26 Nahl's Engraving in Varley, *The Legend of Joaquín Murieta,* 72.
26 *The Golden Era,* 27 March 1853.
27 The effects of heat on a severed head explained to me by Fresno County chief forensic pathologist Venu Gopal, and CSUF professor of anthropology Roger LaJeunesse.
27 "The head does not appear natural . . .": *Alta California,* 13 August 1853, quoting the *Stockton Journal* of the previous day.
28 "A profusion of jet black hair . . .": *Sacramento Daily Union,* 10 September 1853.
28 Frank Marryat: in Secrest, "The Horrifying History of a Highwayman's Head," 28–34.
29 Samuel Bishop's testimony: in Latta, *Joaquín Murrieta and His Horse Gangs,* 588–92.
29–30 The sketch from *Overland Monthly* is reproduced in Boessenecker, *Gold Dust and Gunsmoke,* 87.
30 "flat-nosed Mexican": Cunningham, *The Truth about Murietta,* 15, 110–11.
30 Old-time *vaqueros:* Steiner, "On the Trail of Joaquin Murieta," 66.
30 George Barron: in "Joaquin Murieta Lore," *Western Folklore* 8 (1949), 272.
30 Charles Gottschalk: Wood, *Tales of Old Calaveras,* 87.

History

32 Thomas Larkin: in Pitt, *Decline of the Californios,* i.
32 Nephew of Mariano Vallejo: Guadalupe Vallejo, in DeNevi, *Sketches of Early California,* 3ff; Dana, *Two Years Before the Mast,* 206; Heath, in *Sketches of Early California,* 38.
33 "recklessness and swagger . . .": Starr, *Americans and the California Dream,* 50.
34 Bancroft, "from a wilderness . . .": in Starr, *Americans and the California Dream,* 125.
34 Bancroft: *California Pastoral,* 135, 136, 138, 150; *California Inter Pocula,* 1; *Essays and Miscellany,* 420, 435; *Retrospection,* 232, 239, 234.

35 Vizcaíno: in Beebe and Senkewicz, *Lands of Promise and Despair,* 43.
36 Father Jeronimo Boscana: in Loftis, *California,* 10.
36 Number of land grants: in Holliday, *Rush for Riches,* 24.
37 William Tecumseh Sherman: *Memoirs,* 45.
37 "The feel of the eighteenth century . . .": Starr, *Americans and the California Dream,* 23.
37–38 Davis's description: in DeNevi, *Sketches of Early California,* 40.
38 Mariano Vallejo's son: *Romance and History of the California Ranchos,* 67–68
39 Father Duran: in Heizer and Almquist, *The Other Californians,* 17.
39 Señora Vallejo's servants: in Cleland, *The Cattle on a Thousand Hills,* 31.
39 George Simpson and James Clyman: in Heizer and Almquist, *The Other Californians,* 19.
39–40 Father Junípero Serra: in Holliday, *Rush for Riches,* 10.
40 friar's letter, "succor for these missions . . .": in Richman, *California under Spain and Mexico,* 186.
40 "a society without schools . . .": Starr, *Americans and the California Dream,* 5.
40 "the end of the world": Agustín Janssens in Pitt, *Decline of the Californios,* 5.
40 Forbes, "hopeless crusade": in Kirsch and Murphy, *West of the West,* 173.
40–41 Wilkes, "a total absence . . .": in Kirsch and Murphy, *West of the West,* 207.
41 Juan Bautista Alvarado: in Schwartz, *From West to East,* 64–65.
42 Gov. Arrillaga: in Richman, *California under Spain and Mexico,* 202.
43 "nothing is more common . . .": Richard Henry Dana, *Two Years Before the Mast,* 96.
44 "men of roistering temper": Richman, *California under Spain and Mexico,* 265.
44 "a rough set": Kirsch and Murphy, *West of the West,* 261.
44 "insulting familiarity": Bancroft, *History of California,* vol. 4, 3.
45 Larkin: in Starr, *Americans and the California Dream,* 13.
46 Bidwell: in DeNevi, *Sketches of Early California,* 49.
46 Thompson: in Richman, *California under Spain and Mexico,* 302.
46 Hastings: in Loftis, *California: Where the Twain Did Meet,* 54.
46–47 These 18th-century cultural stereotypes defined in Landes, *The Wealth and Poverty of Nations,* 174.
47 Salazar and Señan: in Richman, *California under Spain and Mexico,* 171.
47 Costansó: in Harlow, *California Conquered,* 32.

47 Geroge Vancouver: in Kirsch and Murphy, *West of the West,* 116, 128, 131.
47 Shaler: in Kirsch and Murphy, *West of the West,* 143, 144.
48 Beechey and Morrell: in Richman, *California under Spain and Mexico,* 299–300.
48 "The men are thriftless . . .": Dana, *Two Years Before the Mast,* 215–16.
48 Colvocoresses: in Starr, *Americans and the California Dream,* 17.
48 Sir George Simpson: in Kirsch and Murphy, *West of the West,* 215.
48 Hastings: in Moses Rischin, "Continuities and Discontinuities in Spanish-Speaking California," 54.
48 Farnham: in Heizer and Almquist, *The Other Californians,* 140.
48–49 Marx: in Schwartz, *From West to East,* 82.
49 Rezanoff: in Richman, *California under Spain and Mexico,* 195.
49 "De Mofras dreamed . . .": Starr, *Americans and the California Dream,* 10.
49 De Mofras quoted in Richman, *California under Spain and Mexico,* 299.
49–50 Vallejo and Thompson: in Richman, *California under Spain and Mexico,* 299, 302.
50 Sir George Simpson: in Richman, *California under Spain and Mexico,* 297.
51 Walpole: in Kirsch and Murphy, *West of the West,* 260.
52 Stearns: in Rosenus, *General M. G. Vallejo and the Advent of the Americans,* 70.
53 "vain, tactless . . .": Bauer, *The Mexican War,* 174.
53 Captain Gillespie: in Harlow, *California Conquered,* 160.
53 Larkin, "It appears . . .": in Harlow, *California Conquered,* 161.
54 Bayard Taylor: in Heizer and Almquist, *The Other Californians,* 142.
55 Taylor's prediction: *Eldorado,* 110.
55 Jones, "whirlwind of anarchy": in Kirsch and Murphy, *West of the West,* 297.
55 "fog, fleas . . .": Cyrille Pierre Théodore Laplace, quoted in Bancroft, *History of California,* vol. 4, 153.
56 Taylor, "unreal and fantastic": in Kirsch and Murphy, *West of the West,* 306.
56 Larkin and inflation: Kirsch and Murphy, *West of the West,* 297.
56–57 Taylor, "in whose embrowned . . .": in Kirsch and Murphy, *West of the West,* 302.
57 Rosales: in Lopez, "The Chileans in the California Gold Rush," 30.
57 "rowdy and knavish . . .": Soulé, Gihon and Nisbet, *The Annals of San Francisco,* 553, 365.

57 Hugo Reid, "vagabonds . . .": in Pitt, *Decline of the Californios,* 52.
57 Delano, Emerson and Colton: in Starr, *Americans and the California Dream,* 58, 66, 31.
58 Taylor, "the magnetism . . .": in Kirsch and Murphy, *West of the West,* 304.
58 "a Homeric world . . .": Starr, *Americans and the California Dream,* 51.
58 *Los Angeles Star:* in Cleland, *The Cattle on a Thousand Hills,* 95.
58–59 Christman: in Starr, *Americans and the California Dream,* 56.
60 Boessenecker: in *Gold Dust and Gunsmoke,* 21.
60 Murray and Miller: in Boessenecker, *Gold Dust and Gunsmoke,* 102–3, 104.
60 Sydney Ducks: in Soulé, Gihon and Nisbet, *The Annals of San Francisco,* 453.
61 Duels: in Soulé, Gihon and Nisbet, *The Annals of San Francisco,* 365.
61 "that delectable crowd . . .": in Holliday, *Rush for Riches,* 201.
61 "official rottenness . . .": *Alta California,* November 1, 1852.
61 "a poor week for killing . . .": in Nadeau, *The Real Joaquín Murieta,* 23.
61–62 Murder rates: in Boessenecker, *Gold Dust and Gunsmoke,* 322–24; 1998 murder rates from U.S. Federal Bureau of Investigation, *Crime in the United States.*
62 Vallejo, "most of the young . . .": in Padilla, *My History, Not Yours,* 101.
63 The story of the Flores-Daniel gang told by Boessenecker, *Gold Dust and Gunsmoke,* 117–33, quotation on 120.
64 *Los Angeles Star:* in Boessenecker, *Gold Dust and Gunsmoke,* 131.
64 Rancheria Massacre: Boessenecker, *Gold Dust and Gunsmoke,* 52–58.
65 "Mexicans were nearly . . .": Pitt, *Decline of the Californios,* 174, 147.
65 "Race categories . . .": Haas, *Conquest and Historical Identities,* 31.
65–66 Ignacio Sepulveda: in Haas, *Conquest and Historical Identities,* 37.
66 Taylor: in *Eldorado,* 109; Soulé, Gihon and Nisbet, *The Annals of San Francisco,* 472; Dana, *Two Years Before the Mast,* 213.
66 Ethnic variety in the Gold Rush: Sucheng Chan, "Ethnic Diversity, Nativism, and Racism," 57.
67 De la Guerra: in Loftis, *California—Where the Twain Did Meet,* 64–65.
67 Californio delegate: in Heizer and Almquist, *The Other Californians,* 98.
67 Bear-and-bull fight: in Johnson, *Roaring Camp,* 182.
67 "The true Germans . . .": Soulé, Gihon and Nisbet, *The Annals of San Francisco,* 464–65.
67 "Jack Rowdy": in Boessenecker, *Gold Dust and Gunsmoke,* 52.

67–68 "disgraceful acts" . . . : *Daily Alta California,* 16 July 1852.
68 Stephen Spencer Hill and Miwok expedition: in Johnson, *Roaring Camp,* 191, 221.
69 Alonzo Delano: in Varley, *The Legend of Joaquin Murrieta,* 13.
69 "The murder of . . .": Boessenecker, *Gold Dust and Gunsmoke,* 133.
70 Colonel Thomas Jefferson Green: in Loftis, *California—Where the Twain Did Meet,* 108.
70 Coronel memoirs: in Richard H. Morefield, "Mexicans in the California Mines," 39.
71 Benjamin Harris, "the foreigners . . .": in Johnson, *Roaring Camp,* 212.
71 Theodore Johnson and proclamation: in Johnson, *Roaring Camp,* 193.
72 Proclamation and *Alta California* editorial: in Hine and Faragher, *The American West: A New Interpretive History,* 244–45.
72 Perkins and *Stockton Times* editorial: in Johnson, *Roaring Camp,* 211, 214.
73 Sacramento editorial on divine sanction: in Gordon, *Joaquin Murieta: Fact, Fiction and Folklore,* 193.
73 Keegan on Great Plains: in *Fields of Battle,* 313.
73 "The farms in the 1850s . . .": Holliday, *Rush for Riches,* 197.
74 1,500 squatters: in Holliday, *Rush for Riches,* 200.
74 "old rancheros . . .": *Alta California,* 1 August 1853.
74 Rancho San Antonio: in Pitt, *Decline of the Californios,* 90.
74 Don Simeon Castro: in Smith, *Garden of the Sun,* 109.
74–75 Data on land commission: Caughey, *California: A Remarkable State's Life History,* 245.
75 Lawyers' fees: in Pitt, *Decline of the Californios,* 94.
75 William Tecumseh Sherman: in Holliday, *Rush for Riches,* 201.
75 European immigrants' land ownership: in Haas, *Conquest and Historical Identity,* 67.

Myth

79 Four-Fingered Jack: *Alta California,* 8 August 1853.
79 Guerillas: Johannsen, *To the Halls of Montezuma,* 36–37.
80 Love interview: *San Joaquin Republican,* 11 August 1853.
80 *Calaveras Chronicle:* in Varley, *The Legend of Joaquín Murrieta,* 49–50.
80 New details: *San Joaquin Republican,* 23 February 1853; 2 March 1853.
83 *New York Tribune:* in Gordon, *Joaquin Murieta,* 202.
84 Sales figures for *Angela the Orphan:* Louis, *Fiction for the Working*

Man, 29; penny dreadfuls: Haining, *The Penny Dreadful.*

85 Ainsworth and *Jack Sheppard:* Worth, *William Harrison Ainsworth.*

85 San Francisco periodicals: Walker, *San Francisco's Literary Frontier,* 14, 24.

86 *California Police Gazette:* Francis Farquhar, "Notes on Joaquin Murieta," in Clough, *Joaquin Murieta: The Brigand Chief of California,* vi.

86 *Sacramento Daily Union,* 16 February 1853: in Varley, *The Legend of Joaquín Murrieta,* 56.

86 "romantic chieftain": *Alta California,* 1 August 1853.

86ff. Details of Ridge's life in Parrins, *John Rollin Ridge;* "eternal shadow" quotation on 30.

87 "deep-seated principle of revenge": in Parrins, *John Rollin Ridge,* 56.

88ff. Ridge, *The Life of Joaquín Murieta,* 7.

90 *Shirley Letters:* Dame Shirley, *California in 1851: The Letters of Dame Shirley,* 74–75.

91 Diamond Springs: Varley, *The Legend of Joaquín Murrieta,* 200 n.19.

91 *Rob Roy* sales figures: in John Lauber, *Sir Walter Scott,* 98.

92 Murieta compared with Three-Fingered Jack: *San Joaquin Republican,* 6 August 1853.

93 *Daily California Chronicle,* 7 August 1854.

93 Ridge letter: Parrins, *John Rollin Ridge,* 106.

94 Howe's play: in *California Gold Rush Plays,* 23–61.

96f. Information on Miller from Frost, *Joaquin Miller.*

97 *Westminster Review:* in Frost, *Joaquin Miller,* 73.

99 1870s: in Starr, *Americans and the California Dream,* 132.

99 Highland Scots: Hugh Trevor-Roper, "The Highland Tradition of Scotland," 25.

101 Horace Bell, *Reminiscences of a Ranger,* 99, 100, 175–76, 185.

102 John Charles Frémont, *Memoirs of My Life,* 370, 376, 409.

102–3 Edwin A. Sherman: "Sherman Was There: The Recollections of Major Edwin A. Sherman," 369.

103 Anecdote about the mortgage: Gordon, *Joaquin Murieta,* 68.

103 Beale: in Bonsal, *Edward Fitzgerald Beale,* 136–39, 279.

104 Hubert Howe Bancroft, *California Pastoral,* 643, 651, 667.

104 Theodore H. Hittell, *History of California,* 713, 725.

105 "a people's champion": Richard E. Meyer, "The Outlaw," 94.

105 Harry Love: in Varley, *The Legend of Joaquín Murrieta,* 127.

105 Byrnes,"one pickled head . . .": in Nadeau, *The Real Joaquin Murieta,* 106.

105 Sightings of Murieta: in Secrest, *The Return of Joaquin,* 15; Nadeau, *The Real Joaquin Murieta,* 105.

106 Grave in Sonora: Steiner, "On the Trail of Joaquin Murieta," 66.

106 B. F. Marshall: the *Stockton Record,* 3 September 1932. Photographic process: O. Henry Mace, *Between the Rivers,* 17. Further information about Marshall: Latta, *Joaquin Murrieta and his Horse Gangs,* 286–99.

107–8 Treasure: Nadeau, *The Real Joaquin Murieta,* 129–31, 133; Gordon, *Joaquin Murieta: Fact, Fiction, and Folklore,* 84–85; 130–35; Jackson, *Bad Company,* 24.

108–9 Mariana la Loca: Raymund Wood, *Mariana la Loca.*

109–10 Owens's diary: Raymund Wood, "New Light on Joaquin Murrieta," 54–65.

110 Spanish-language versions: Leal, "Introducción," 21–25.

112 "fantasy heritage": McWilliams, *North from Mexico,* 35.

112 Ramona and the *Mission Play:* Starr, *Inventing the Dream,* 60–63, 87–89.

112 Santa Barbara and San Francisco plays: Varley, *The Legend of Joaquín Murrieta,* 150.

113 Tinkham, *California Men and Events,* 129, 131; circus: Henshall, "A Bandit of the Golden Age," 313.

113 Mitchell M. A. thesis, *Joaquin Murieta,* 38.

113 Bechdolt: in Jackson, *Bad Company,* 30.

114 "merry moods: Corcoran, "Robber Joaquin," 4.

114 Jackson: Introduction to reprint of Ridge, *Joaquin Murieta,* xliii.

115–17 Ranger William Howard: Cossley-Batt, *Last of the California Rangers,* 159, 161, 167, 168, 175.

117 Bell, *On the Old West Coast,* 33–35.

117f. Carillo: in Leal, "Introducción," 45–47.

119–20 Burns, *The Robin Hood of El Dorado,* 40, 26, 30, 41, 47, 42, 43.

120 Reviews: *New York Times,* 17 April 1932; *Books,* February 1932.

120ff. Mexicans in film: Keller, *Hispanics and United States Film,* 14.

122 Zorro: Keller, *Hispanics and United States Film,* 60.

122ff. Film Murietas: Tuska, *The American West in Film,* 197–201.

123 Acevedo play: Leal, "Introducción," 58.

124 Jack as Irish: Woods, *Tales of Old Calaveras,* 81.

126 Corle, "The highwaymen . . .": *The Royal Highway,* 279.

126–28 Allende, *Daughter of Fortune,* 106, 112–13, 59, 107, 100, 307, 338–39, 357, 399.

128–29 Cunningham: Latta, *Joaquin Murrieta and His Horse Gangs,* 265.

130 Jackson: *Bad Company,* 4; Introduction, xi.

130 "cutthroat Mexican bandit . . .": Cleland, *From Wilderness to Empire,* 291.

131 English folksong, "Joaquin the Horsethief": in Hulbert, *Forty-Niners,* 189. Hulbert claims this song was circulating in 1849, which can't be true, since it mentions Lola Montez, who didn't come to California until 1853.

132 Chappo in prison: in Secrest, "The Horrifying History of a Highwayman's Head," 29.

133 Rojas reminiscences: *Last of the Vaqueros,* 134–40.

134 Corridos: Limón, *Mexican Ballads, Chicano Poems,* 9–17; quotation on 24; Leal, "Introducción," 65–79.

134–35 Murieta *corrido:* Sonnichsen, liner notes from Strachwitz, *Texas-Mexican Border Music,* vol. 1 & 2.

135–36 Mexican immigration: McWilliams, *Factories in the Field,* 103–33; *North from Mexico,* 163; Acuña, *Occupied America,* 197.

136 Crusade for Justice: Acuña, *Occupied America,* 371.

137 Gonzales speech: in *Message to Aztlán,* 32. Quotations from the poem are from this edition.

137f. Gonzales poem: Esquibel, "Introduction," xxiv–xxv.

138 Garcia: in *Chicanismo,* 139.

139 Steiner, "Not since the days . . .": in La Raza, 195.

139–40 Neruda, *Passions and Impressions,* 140, 141; *Splendor and Death,* x, 15, 73, 75, 79, 115, 123, 131, 149.

141 1976 version of *corrido:* reproduced in Gordon, *Joaquin Murieta,* 205.

141 "social bandit": Hobsbawm, *Bandits,* 7, 10.

142 "archetypal social bandit . . .": López y Rivas, *Conquest and Rebellion,* 102.

142 "a composite name . . .": Padilla, *My History, Not Yours,* 253 n.212.

142f. Anthology: Valdez and Steiner, *Aztlan,* 105–10.

143 Meier and Ribera, *Mexican Americans/American Mexicans,* 76.

143 "challenged the dominant order": Mirandé, *The Chicano Experience,* 73.

143 Vigil, *From Indians to Chicanos,* 157.

143 Acuña, *Occupied America,* 147, 149.

143–44 Vélez-Ibáñez, *Border Visions,* 100, 101, 102, 265.

144 Del Castillo, "Joaquin Murrieta," in Etulain and Riley, *With Badges and Bullets,* 106, 111, 107; Rojas, *Joaquín Murrieta, "El Patrio,"* 14, 16, 23, 38.

144 Rawls and Bean, *California: An Interpretive History,* 148, 151.

145 "fragility of the evidence": Wyatt, *Five Fires,* 67, 71.

145 "heroic myth": Schwartz, *From East to West,* 81, 82.

145 "provide for the poor": Hine and Faracher, *The American West,* ix, 213, 214.

145 "a denial . . .": Himmelfarb, "Postmodernist History," *On Looking into the Abyss,* 133.

146 "to interrogate . . .": Johnson, *Roaring Camp,* 11, 12, 13, 14, 28; Latta, *Joaquín Murrieta and His Horse Gangs,* 593.

146–48 Powell, "Historical Multiculturalism," 186, 187, 193; Powell, *Ruthless Democracy,* 73.

148ff. History of Murieta's head: Varley, *The Legend of Joaquín Murrieta,* 170–71; William B. Secrest, *The Return of Joaquin,* 22–23, and *Joaquin: Bloody Bandit of the Motherlode,* 40.

148 Crowd at Diamond Springs: Latta, *Joaquín Murrieta and His Horse Gangs,* 596.

148 Daggett, "We question . . .": Varley, *The Legend of Joaquín Murrieta,* 128.

148 Chiles: Varley, *The Legend of Joaquín Murrieta,* 134.

148 Head and hand stolen: Corle, *The Royal Highway,* 277.

149 Natchez and ghost story: Bell, *On the Old West Coast,* 32–35.

149 Craigmiles: Varley, *The Legend of Joaquín Murrieta,* 171.

150 Dr. Jordan's Pacific Museum: Latta, *Joaquín Murrieta and His Horse Gangs,* 600–2, 612–16

150 Charles Bull: in Secrest, "The Horrifying History of a Highwayman's Head."

150–51 Latta's claim: in *Joaquín Murrieta and His Horse Gangs,* 616.

151 Johnson's head: Gordon, *Murieta: Fact, Fiction and Folklore,* 158–59; Secrest, "The Horrifying History of a Highwayman's Head."

152 Rojas, "bitter memories": in Valdez and Steiner, *Aztlan,* 108.

152 Head and hand: *San Francisco Chronicle,* 30 April 1980.

152–53 Rodriguez, *Days of Obligation,* 133–48.

The Ride Back to Three Rocks

157 "contributions" or "spirit": "Spirit of the Ride," *Fresno Bee,* 28 July 2001, B1–B4.

BIBLIOGRAPHY

I am particularly indebted to James Varley's *The Legend of Joaquín Murrieta* and John Boessenecker's *Gold Dust and Gunsmoke.*

Acuña, Rodolfo. *Occupied America: A History of Chicanos.* 4th edition. New York, 2000.

Aguirre Bernal, Celso. *Joaquin Murrieta: Raiz y Razón del Movimiento Chicano: Un Efoque Histórico.* México, DF, 1985.

Allende, Isabel. *Daughter of Fortune.* New York, 1999.

Atherton, Gertrude Franklin Horn. *The Splendid Idle Forties: Stories of California.* New York, 1902.

Badger, Joseph. *Joaquin, the Terrible: The True History of the Three Bitter Blows That Changed an Honest Man to a Merciless Demon.* Brooklyn, N.Y., 1947.

Bancroft, Hubert Howe. *California Inter Pocula.* San Francisco, 1888.

Bancroft, Hubert Howe. *California Pastoral, 1769–1848.* San Francisco, 1888.

Bancroft, Hubert Howe. *Essays and Miscellany.* San Francisco, 1888.

Bancroft, Hubert Howe. *History of California.* Vol. 5, 1846–48. Santa Barbara, 1963–1970.

Bancroft, Hubert Howe. *Retrospections.* New York, 1912.

Barron, Joseph. "Joaquin Murieta Lore." *Western Folklore* 8 (1949): 272.

Bartlett, Lanier, and Virginia Stivers Bartlett. *Adiós!* New York, 1929.

Bauer, K. Jack. *The Mexican War, 1846–1848.* New York, 1974.

Beebe, Rose Marie, and Robert M. Senkewicz. *Lands of Promise and Despair.* Santa Clara, 2001.

Beilharz, Edwin A., and Carlos V. López, eds. *We Were the 49ers!: Chilean Accounts of the California Gold Rush.* Pasadena, Calif., 1976.

Bell, Horace. *On the Old West Coast: Being Further Reminiscences of a Ranger, Major Horace Bell.* New York, 1930.

Bell, Horace. *Reminiscences of a Ranger: Or, Early Times in Southern California.* Los Angeles, 1881.

Berumen, Frank Javier Garcia. *The Chicano/Hispanic Image in American Film.* New York, 1995.

Bidwell, John. *A Journey to California, 1841: The First Emigrant Party to California by Wagon Train; The Journal of John Bidwell.* Berkeley, 1964.

Blew, Robert. "The Californios and American Society." *The Californians* 3:3 (1985): 15–18.

Boessenecker, John. *Gold Dust and Gunsmoke: Tales of Gold Rush Outlaws, Gunfighters, Lawmen, and Vigilantes.* New York, 1999.

Bonsal, Stephen. *Edward Fitzgerald Beale, a Pioneer in the Path of Empire, 1822–1903.* New York and London, 1912.

Burns, Walter Noble. *The Robin Hood of El Dorado: The Saga of Joaquin Murrieta, Famous Outlaw of California's Age of Gold.* New York, 1932.

Caughey, John Watson. *California: A Remarkable State's Life History.* Englewood Cliffs, N.J., 1970.

Cleland, Robert Glass. *The Cattle on a Thousand Hills: Southern California, 1850–1870.* San Marion, Calif., 1941.

Cleland, Robert Glass. *From Wilderness to Empire: A History of California, 1542–1900.* New York, 1944.

Clough, Charles. *Joaquin Murieta, the Brigand Chief of California: A Complete History of His Life from the Age of Sixteen to the Time of His Capture and Death in 1853.* Fresno, Calif., 1969.

Coolidge, Dane. *Gringo Gold: A Story of Joaquin Murieta, the Bandit.* New York, 1939.

Corcoran, May S. "Robber Joaquin: As Seen in Statues of California Legislature Journals and One Living Ranger." *Grizzly Bear.* Los Angeles, 1921.

Corle, Edwin. *The Royal Highway (El Camino Real).* Indianapolis, 1949.

Cossley-Batt, Jill L. *The Last of the California Rangers.* New York and London, 1928.

Crosby, Harry. *Last of the Californios.* La Jolla, Calif., 1981.

Cunningham, James. *The Truth about Murietta: Anecdotes and Facts Related by Those Who Knew Him and Disbelieve His Capture.* Los Angeles, 1938.

Curtis, Sandra. *Zorro Unmasked: The Official History.* New York, 1998.

Dana, Richard Henry, Jr. *Two Years Before the Mast, and Twenty-four Years After.* Los Angeles, 1964.

DeNevi, Don. *Sketches of Early California: A Collection of Personal Adventures.* San Francisco, 1971.

Dickson, Samuel. *Tales of San Francisco.* Stanford, Calif., 1957.

Duke, Thomas. *Celebrated Criminal Cases of America.* San Francisco, 1910.

Etulain, Richard W., and Glenda Riley. *With Badges and Bullets: Lawmen and Outlaws of the Old West.* Golden, Col., 1999.

Fleischman, Sid. *Bandit's Moon.* New York, 1998.

Frémont, John Charles. *Memoirs of My Life.* Chicago and New York, 1887.

Frost, Orcutt William. *Joaquin Miller.* New York, 1967.

Gaffey, Shirley. "California Land Grant Disputes, 1852–72: A Rhetorical Analysis." Dissertation, University of Southern California, 1975.

Garcia, Ignacio. *Chicanismo.* Tucson, 1997.

Garrison, Myrtle. *Romance and History of the California Ranchos.* San Francisco, 1935.

Glasscock, Carl B. *A Golden Highway.* New York, 1934.

Gollomb, Joseph. *Master Man Hunters.* New York, 1926.

Gonzales, Rodolpho. *Message to Aztlán.* Houston, 2001.

Gordon, Thomas J. *Joaquin Murieta: Fact, Fiction, and Folklore.* Dissertation, Utah University, 1983.

Gray, Carl. *A Plaything of the Gods.* Boston, 1912.

Guinn, J. M. *History of the State of California and Biographical Record of the San Joaquin Valley.* California and Chicago, 1905.

Gutiérrez, Ramón, and Richard Orsi. *Contested Eden: California Before the Gold Rush.* Berkeley, 1998.

Gwaltney, Don. *The Bandit Joaquin: An Orphaned Mexican's Search for Revenge in the California Gold Rush.* Worthbrook, Ill., 1997.

Haas, Lisbeth. *Conquest and Historical Identities in California, 1769–1936.* Berkeley, 1995.

Hadley-Garcia, George. *Hispanic Hollywood: The Latins in Motion Pictures.* New York, 1990.

Hainig, Peter. *The Penny Dreadful: Or, Strange, Horrid and Sensational Tales!* London, 1975.

Heizer, Robert Fleming, and Alan Almquist. *The Other Californians: Prejudice and Discrimination under Spain, Mexico and the United States to 1920.* Berkeley, 1971.

Henshall, John A. "A Bandit of the Golden Age." *Overland Monthly,* 1909: 313–19.

Henshall, John A. "Tales of the Early California Bandits." *Overland Monthly,* 1909.

Himmelfarb, Gertrude. *On Looking into the Abyss: Untimely Thoughts on Culture and Society.* New York, 1994.

Hine, Robert, and John Mack Faragher. *The American West: A New Interpretative History.* New Haven and London, 2000.

Hobsbawm, Eric. *Bandits.* London, 2000.

Holliday, J. S. *Rush for Riches: Gold Fever and the Making of California.* Berkeley, 1999.

Howe, Charles E. B. "Joaquin Murieta de Castillo." In *California Gold-Rush Plays.* Edited by Glenn Loney. New York, 1983.

Huerta, Father Alberto. "Joaquin Murieta: Califoria's Literary Archetype." *The Californians* 5 (1987): 46–50.

Hulbert, Archer Butler. *Forty-niners: The Chronicle of the California Trail.* Boston, 1901.

Hunt, Rockwell Dennis. *Oxcart to Airplane.* Los Angeles, 1929–1931.

Jackson, Joseph Henry. *Bad Company.* New York, 1949.

Jackson, Joseph Henry. "The Creation of Joaquin Murieta." *Pacific Spectator* 2 (1948): 176–81.

James, Louis. *Fiction for the Working Man, 1830–1850: A Study of the Literature Produced for the Working Classes in Early Victorian Urban England.* London and New York, 1963.

Johannsen, Robert. *To the Halls of the Montezumas.* New York, 1983.

Johnson, Susan. *Roaring Camp: The Social World of the California Gold Rush.* New York and London, 2000.

Keegan, John. *Fields of Battle.* New York, 1995.

Keller, Gary. *Hispanics and United States Film.* Tempe, Ariz., 1994.

Kirsch, Robert, and William S. Murphy. *West of the West: Witnesses to the California Experience, 1542–1906: The Story of California from the Conquistadors to the Great Earthquake.* New York, 1967.

Klette, Ernest. *The Crimson Trail of Joaquin Murieta.* Los Angeles, 1928.

Klyn, Dianne C. *Joaquin Murieta in California.* San Ramon, Calif., 1989.

Lampson, Robin. *San Francisco Souvenir.* San Francisco, 1938.

Landes, David. *The Wealth and Poverty of Nations.* New York and London, 1998.

Lang, Margaret Hanna. *Early Justice in Sonora.* Sonora, Calif., 1963.

Lape, Noreen Groover. *West of the Border: The Multicultural Literature of the Western American Frontiers.* Athens, Georgia, 2000.

Latta, Frank. *Joaquín Murrieta and His Horse Gangs.* Santa Cruz, Calif., 1980.

Lauber, John. *Sir Walter Scott.* New York, 1966.

Lavender, David Sievert. *California: Land of New Beginnings.* New York, 1972.

Leal, Luis. "Introducción." *Vida y Aventuras del Más Célebre Bandido Sonorense, Joaquín Murrieta: y sus Grandes Proezas en el Estado de California.* Houston, 1999.

Lee, Hector. "Joaquin Murieta." *Quarterly of the National Association and Center for Outlaw and Lawman History* 5:4 (1981): 17–20.

Lee, Hector. "The Reverberant Joaquin Murieta in California Legendry." *Pacific Historian* 25:3 (1987): 38–47.

Lee, Hector. *Tales of California from the History and Folklore of the Far West.* Santa Rosa, Calif., 1974.

Limón, José Eduardo. *Mexican Ballads, Chicano Poems: History and Influence in Mexican-American Social Poetry.* Berkeley, 1992.

Loftis, Anne. *California—Where the Twain Did Meet.* New York, 1973.

López y Rivas, Gilberto. *Conquest and Resistance: The Origins of the Chicano National Minority.* Palo Alto, Calif., 1979.

Mace, O. Henry. *Between the Rivers: History of Early Calaveras County.* 2nd edition. Sutter Creek and Jackson, Calif., 1993.

MacLean, Angus. *Legends of the California Bandidos.* Fresno, 1977.

Martínez, Gilbert. *The Mexican American: His Life across Four Centuries.* Boston, 1973.

Mason, Jesse. *History of Amador County, California.* Volcano, Calif., 1968.

McCarthy, Gary. *The Gringo Amigo.* New York, 1991.

McWilliams, Carey. *Factories in the Field: The Story of Migratory Farm Labor in California.* Boston, 1939.

McWilliams, Carey. *North from Mexico.* New York. 1968.

Meyer, Richard E. "The Outlaw: A Distinctive American Folklore." *Journal of the Folklore Institute* 17:2–3 (1980): 94–124.

Miller, Joaquin. *Songs of the Sierras and the Sunlands.* Chicago, 1893.

Miller, Mary Merril. *Mother Lode, 1849–1949.* Culver City, Calif., 1949.
Mirandé, Alfredo. *The Chicano Experience: An Alternative Perspective.* Notre Dame, Ind., 1985.
Mitchell, Richard Gerald. "Joaquin Murieta: A Study of Social Conditions in Early California." MA Thesis, UCLA, 1926.
Morefield, Richard H. "Mexicans in the California Mines." *California Historical Society Quarterly* 35 (1956): 37–46.
Nadeau, Remi A. *The Real Joaquin Murieta: Robin Hood Hero or Gold Rush Gangster?* Corona del Mar, Calif., 1974.
Nava, Julian. *Viva la Raza: Readings on Mexican Americans.* New York, 1973.
Neruda, Pablo. *Fulgor y Muerte de Joaquín Murieta, Bandido Chileno Injusticiado en California el 23 de Julio de 1853.* Santiago de Chile, 1967.
Neruda, Pablo. *Passions and Impressions.* New York, 1983.
Neruda, Pablo. *Splendor and Death of Joaquin Murieta.* New York, 1972.
Nevins, Allan. *Frémont, Pathmaker of the West.* New York, 1955.
Padillo, Genaro M. *My History, Not Yours: The Formation of Mexican American Autobiography.* Madison, Wis., 1993.
Parins, James. *John Rollin Ridge: His Life and Works.* Lincoln, 1991.
Paz, Ireneo. *Vida y Aventuras del Más Célebre Bandido Sonorense, Joaquín Murrieta: y sus Grandes Proezas en el Estado de California.* Los Angeles, 1919.
Pedro, Castillo. *Furia y Muerte: Los Bandidos Chicanos.* Los Angeles, 1973.
Peeples, Samuel Anthony. *The Dream Ends in Fury: A Novel Based on the Life of Joaquin Murrieta.* New York, 1949.
Peterson, Richard. "Anti-Mexican Nativism in California, 1848–1853: A Study of Cultural Conflict." *California Historical Society Quarterly* 62 (1980): 309–27.
Peterson, Richard. "The Foreign Miner's Tax of 1850 and Mexicans in California: Exploitation or Expulsion?" *Pacific Historian* 20:3 (1976): 265–72.
Peterson, Richard. *Manifest Destiny in the Mines: A Cultural Interpretation of Anti-Mexican Nativism in California, 1848–1853.* San Francisco, 1975.
Pitt, Leonard. *Decline of the Californios.* Berkeley, 1966.
Powell, Timothy, editor. *Beyond the Binary: Reconstructing Cultural Identity in a Multicultural Context.* New Brunswick, N.J., 1999.

Powell, Timothy. *Ruthless Democracy: A Multicultural Interpretation of the American Renaissance.* Princeton, 2000.

Rawls, James, and Walton Bean. *California: An Interpretive History.* New York, 1998.

Reynolds, David. *Beneath the American Renaissance: The Subversive Imagination in the Age of Emerson and Melville.* New York, 1988.

Richard, Alfred Charles. *Censorship and Hollywood's Hispanic Image: An Interpretive Filmography, 1936–55.* Westport, Conn., 1993.

Richman, Irving Berdine. *California under Spain and Mexico, 1535–1847.* Boston and New York, 1911.

Robinson, W. W. *Land in California: The Story of Mission Lands, Ranchos, Squatters, Mining Claims, Railroad Grants, Land Scrip Homesteads.* Berkeley, 1948.

Rodriguez, Richard. *Days of Obligation: An Argument with My Mexican Father.* New York, 1992.

Rohrbough, Malcolm J. *Days of Gold: The California Gold Rush and the American Nation.* Berkeley, 1997.

Rojas, Arnold R. *Last of the Vaqueros.* Fresno, Calif., 1960.

Rojas, Manuel. *Joaquín Murrieta, el Patrio: El "Far West" del México cercenado.* Mexicali, Mexico, 1990.

Rojas, Manuel. *Joaquín Murrieta, el Patrio: Truthful Focuses for the Chicano Movement.* Blythe, Calif., 1996.

Romero, Michael. *Joaquin Murrieta: The Life of a Legend.* Soledad, Calif., 1979.

Rosenbaum, Robert. *Mexican Resistance in the Southwest: "The Sacred Right of Self-Preservation."* Austin, 1981.

Rosenus, Alan. *General M. G. Vallejo and the Advent of the Americans: A Biography.* Albuquerque, 1995.

Salinas, Luis Omar, and Lillian Faderman, editors. *From the Barrio: A Chicano Anthology.* San Fransisco, 1973.

Sante, Luc. *Low Life: Lures and Snares of Old New York.* New York, 1991.

Schwartz, Stephen. *From West to East: California and the Making of the American Mind.* New York, 1998.

Secrest, William. *California Desperadoes: Stories of Early California Outlaws in Their Own Words.* Clovis, Calif., 2000.

Secrest, William. "The Horrifying History of a Highwayman's Head." *The Californians,* 4.6 (1986): 28–34.

Secrest, William. *Joaquin: Bloody Bandit of the Motherlode.* Fresno, Calif., 1967.

Secrest, William. *The Return of Joaquin.* Fresno, Calif., 1973.

Sherman, William T. *The Memoirs of General W. T. Sherman.* 1891. Reprint: New York, 1990.

"Sherman Was There: The Recollections of Major Edwin A. Sherman." *California Historical Society Quarterly* 23:4 (1944).

Shirley, Dame (Louise Clappe). *California in 1851: The Letters of Dame Shirley.* Reprint: San Franciso, 1933.

Smith, Wallace. *Garden of the Sun.* Fresno, Calif., 1960.

Snow, Charles. *The Sheriff of Chispa Loma.* Philadelphia, 1931.

Soulé, Frank, John H. Gihon, and James Nisbet. *The Annals of San Francisco.* 1855. Reprint, Palo Alto, 1966.

Starr, Kevin. *Americans and the California Dream, 1850–1915.* New York, 1973.

Starr, Kevin. *Inventing the Dream.* New York, 1985.

Steckmesser, Kent. "Joaquin Murieta and Billy the Kid." *Western Folklore* 21:2 (1962): 77–82.

Steiner, Stan. *La Raza: The Mexican Americans.* New York, 1970.

Steiner, Stan. "On the Trial of Joaquin Murieta." *American West* 18 (1981): 54–57.

Strachwitz, Chris. *Texas-Mexican Border Music: An Introduction.* Berkeley, 1974.

Taylor, Bayard. *Eldorado; or Adventures in the Path of Empire.* New York, 1949.

Tinkham, George H. *California Men and Events: Time 1769–1890.* Stockton, Calif., 1915.

Trevor-Roper, Hugh. "The Highland Tradition of Scotland." In *The Invention of Tradition.* Edited by E. J. Hobsbawm and T. O. Ranger. Cambridge and New York, 1983.

Tusca, Jon. *The American West in Film.* Westport, Conn., 1985.

Tuthill, Frank. *History of California.* San Francisco, 1866.

Upton, Charles Elmer. *Pioneers of El Dorado.* Placerville, Calif., 1906.

Valdez, Luis, and Stan Steiner. *Aztlan: An Anthology of Mexican American Literature.* New York, 1972.

Valenzuel, Arce, and José Manuel. *Entre la magica y historia.* Tijuana, 1992.

Varley, James. *The Legend of Joaquín Murrieta: California's Gold Rush Bandit.* Twin Falls, Idaho, 1995.

Vélez-Ibanez, Carlos G. *Border Visions: Mexican Cultures of the Southwest United States.* Tucson, 1996.

Walker, Dale. *Bear Flag Rising: The Conquest of California, 1846.* New York, 1999.

Walker, Franklin. "Ridge's Life of Joaquin Murieta. The First and Revised Editions Compared." *California Historical Society Quarterly* 16 (1937): 256–61.

Wellman, William. *A Short Time for Insanity: An Autobiography by William A. Wellman.* New York, 1974.

Wood, R. Coke. *Tales of Old Calaveras.* Angels Camp, Calif., 1949.

Wood, Raymund F. "Mariana Andrada in California." *Pacific Historian* 16:3 (1972): 77–81.

Wood, Raymund F. *Mariana la Loca.* Fresno, Calif., 1970.

Wood, Raymund F. "New Light on Joaquin Murrieta." *Pacific Historian* 14:1 (1970): 54–64.

Worth, George. *William Harrison Ainsworth.* New York, 1972.

Wyatt, David. *Five Fires.* Reading, Mass., 1997.

Index